The Ultimate ECAA Guide

UniAdmissions

Published by RAR Medical Services Limited trading as **Infinity Books Ltd**
www.uniadmissions.co.uk
info@uniadmissions.co.uk
Tel: 0208 068 0438

The Ultimate ECAA Guide
300 Practice Questions

David Meacham

Rohan Agarwal

UniAdmissions

About the Author

David is a **Merger & Acquisitions Associate** at The Hut Group, a leading online retailer and brand owner in the Beauty & Wellness sectors. Prior to joining The Hut Group, he worked in roles at the Professional Service firm Deloitte, the Investment Bank Greenhill and the Private Equity firm Hgcapital.

David graduated with a **first class honours** in Economics from Gonville and Caius College Cambridge, where he received two college scholarships for outstanding academic performance, in addition to an Essay Prize. He is also a qualified accountant and chartered tax adviser, passing all exams first-time with multiple regional top scores. Since graduating, David has tutored & successfully provided academic coaching to hundreds of students, both in a personal capacity and for university admissions.

Rohan is the **Director of Operations** at *UniAdmissions* and is responsible for its technical and commercial arms. He graduated from Gonville and Caius College, Cambridge and is a fully qualified doctor. Over the last five years, he has tutored hundreds of successful Oxbridge and Medical applicants. He has also authored ten books on admissions tests and interviews.

Rohan has taught physiology to undergraduates and interviewed medical school applicants for Cambridge. He has published research on bone physiology and writes education articles for the Independent and Huffington Post. In his spare time, Rohan enjoys playing the piano and table tennis.

Contents

The Basics

What is the ECAA?

The Economics Admissions Assessment (ECAA) is a two-hour written exam for prospective Cambridge Economics applicants.

What does the ECAA consist of?

Section	Skills Tested	Questions	Timing
1A 1B	Mathematics Advanced Mathematics	20 MCQs 20 MCQs	60 minutes (recommend 30 minutes for each)
2	Writing Task	One Long Essay	60 minutes

Why is the ECAA used?

Cambridge applicants tend to be a bright bunch and therefore usually have excellent grades. The majority of economics applicants score in excess of 90% in their A level subjects. This means that competition is fierce – meaning that the universities must use the ECAA to help differentiate between applicants.

When do I sit ECAA?

The ECAA normally takes place in the first week of November every year, normally on a Wednesday Morning.

Can I resit the ECAA?

No, you can only sit the ECAA once per admissions cycle.

Where do I sit the ECAA?

You can usually sit the ECAA at your school or college (ask your exams officer for more information). Alternatively, if your school isn't a registered test centre or you're not attending a school or college, you can sit the ECAA at an authorised test centre.

Who has to sit the ECAA?

All applicants for Cambridge Economics need to sit the test.

Do I have to resit the ECAA if I reapply?

Yes, each admissions cycle is independent - you cannot use your score from any previous attempts.

How is the ECAA Scored?

In section 1, each question carries one mark and there is no negative marking. Both sections 1A + 1B are equally weighted and results are reported separately. In section 2, your answer will be assessed based on the argument and also its clarity.

How is the ECAA used?

Different Cambridge colleges will place different weightings on different components so it's important you find out as much information about how your marks will be used by emailing the college admissions office.

In general, the university will interview a high proportion of realistic applicants so the ECAA score isn't vital for making the interview shortlist. However, it can play a huge role in the final decision after your interview.

General Advice

Start Early

It is much easier to prepare if you practice little and often. Start your preparation well in advance; ideally by mid September but at the latest by early October. This way you will have plenty of time to complete as many papers as you wish to feel comfortable and won't have to panic and cram just before the test, which is a much less effective and more stressful way to learn. In general, an early start will give you the opportunity to identify the complex issues and work at your own pace.

Prioritise

Some questions in sections 1 + 2 can be long and complex – and given the intense time pressure you need to know your limits. It is essential that you don't get stuck with very difficult questions. If a question looks particularly long or complex, mark it for review and move on. You don't want to be caught 5 questions short at the end just because you took more than 3 minutes in answering a challenging multi-step physics question. If a question is taking too long, choose a sensible answer and move on. Remember that each question carries equal weighting and therefore, you should adjust your timing in accordingly. With practice and discipline, you can get very good at this and learn to maximise your efficiency.

Positive Marking

There are no penalties for incorrect answers in the ECAA; you will gain one for each right answer and will not get one for each wrong or unanswered one. This provides you with the luxury that you can always guess should you absolutely be not able to figure out the right answer for a question or run behind time. Since each question provides you with 4 to 6 possible answers, you have a 16-25% chance of guessing correctly. Therefore, if you aren't sure (and are running short of time), then make an educated guess and move on. Before 'guessing' you should try to eliminate a couple of answers to increase your chances of getting the question correct. For example, if a question has 5 options and you manage to eliminate 2 options- your chances of getting the question increase from 20% to 33%!

Avoid losing easy marks on other questions because of poor exam technique. Similarly, if you have failed to finish the exam, take the last 10 seconds to guess the remaining questions to at least give yourself a chance of getting them right.

Practice

This is the best way of familiarising yourself with the style of questions and the timing for this section. Although the ECAA tests only GCSE level knowledge, you are unlikely to be familiar with the style of questions in all 3 sections when you first encounter them. Therefore, you want to be comfortable at using this before you sit the test.

Practising questions will put you at ease and make you more comfortable with the exam. The more comfortable you are, the less you will panic on the test day and the more likely you are to score highly. Initially, work through the questions at your own pace, and spend time carefully reading the questions and looking at any additional data. When it becomes closer to the test, make sure you practice the questions under exam conditions.

Past Papers

The ECAA is a very new exam so there aren't many sample papers available. Specimen papers are freely available online at www.uniadmissions.co.uk/ECAA. Once you've worked your way through the questions in this book, you are highly advised to attempt them.

Repeat Questions

When checking through answers, pay particular attention to questions you have got wrong. If there is a worked answer, look through that carefully until you feel confident that you understand the reasoning, and then repeat the question without help to check that you can do it. If only the answer is given, have another look at the question and try to work out why that answer is correct. This is the best way to learn from your mistakes, and means you are less likely to make similar mistakes when it comes to the test. The same applies for questions which you were unsure of and made an educated guess which was correct, even if you got it right. When working through this book, make sure you highlight any questions you are unsure of, this means you know to spend more time looking over them once marked.

> **Top tip!**
> In general, students tend to improve the fastest in section 2 and slowest in section 1A; section 1B usually falls somewhere in the middle. Thus, if you have very little time left, it's best to prioritise section 2.

No Calculators

You aren't permitted to use calculators in the ECAA – thus, it is essential that you have strong numerical skills. For instance, you should be able to rapidly convert between percentages, decimals and fractions. You will seldom get questions that would require calculators but you would be expected to be able to arrive at a sensible estimate. Consider for example:

Estimate 3.962 x 2.322;

3.962 is approximately 4 and 2.323 is approximately 2.33 = 7/3.

Thus, $3.962 \times 2.322 » 4 \times \frac{7}{3} = \frac{28}{3} = 9.33$

Since you will rarely be asked to perform difficult calculations, you can use this as a signpost of if you are tackling a question correctly. For example, when solving a physics question, you end up having to divide 8,079 by 357- this should raise alarm bells as calculations in the ECAA are rarely this difficult.

A word on timing...

"If you had all day to do your ECAA, you would get 100%. But you don't."

Whilst this isn't completely true, it illustrates a very important point. Once you've practiced and know how to answer the questions, the clock is your biggest enemy. This seemingly obvious statement has one very important consequence. **The way to improve your ECAA score is to improve your speed**. There is no magic bullet. But there are a great number of techniques that, with practice, will give you significant time gains, allowing you to answer more questions and score more marks.

Timing is tight throughout the ECAA – **mastering timing is the first key to success**. Some candidates choose to work as quickly as possible to save up time at the end to check back, but this is generally not the best way to do it. ECAA questions can have a lot of information in them – each time you start answering a question it takes time to get familiar with the instructions and information. By splitting the question into two sessions (the first run-through and the return-to-check) you double the amount of time you spend on familiarising yourself with the data, as you have to do it twice instead of only once. This costs valuable time. In addition, candidates who do check back may spend 2–3 minutes doing so and yet not make any actual changes. Whilst this can be reassuring, it is a false reassurance as it is unlikely to have a significant effect on your actual score. Therefore it is usually best to pace yourself very steadily, aiming to spend the same amount of time on each question and finish the final question in a section just as time runs out. This reduces the time spent on re-familiarising with questions and maximises the time spent on the first attempt, gaining more marks.

It is essential that you don't get stuck with the hardest questions – no doubt there will be some. In the time spent answering only one of these you may miss out on answering three easier questions. If a question is taking too long, choose a sensible answer and move on. Never see this as giving up or in any way failing, rather it is the smart way to approach a test with a tight time limit. With practice and discipline, you can get very good at this and learn to maximise your efficiency. It is not about being a hero and aiming for full marks – this is almost impossible and very much unnecessary (even Oxbridge will regard any score higher than 7 as exceptional). It is about maximising your efficiency and gaining the maximum possible number of marks within the time you have.

Top tip!
Ensure that you take a watch that can show you the time in seconds into the exam. This will allow you have a much more accurate idea of the time you're spending on a question. In general, if you've spent more than 3 minutes on question – move on regardless of how close you think you are to solving it.

Use the Options:

Some questions may try to overload you with information. When presented with large tables and data, it's essential you look at the answer options so you can focus your mind. This can allow you to reach the correct answer a lot more quickly. Consider the example below:

The table below shows the results of a study investigating antibiotic resistance in staphylococcus populations. A single staphylococcus bacterium is chosen at random from a similar population. Resistance to any one antibiotic is independent of resistance to others.

Calculate the probability that the bacterium selected will be resistant to all four drugs.

A. 1 in 10^6
B. 1 in 10^{12}
C. 1 in 10^{20}
D. 1 in 10^{25}
E. 1 in 10^{30}
F. 1 in 10^{35}

Antibiotic	Number of Bacteria tested	Number of Resistant Bacteria
Benzyl-penicillin	10^{11}	98
Chloramphenicol	10^9	1200
Metronidazole	10^8	256
Erythromycin	10^5	2

Looking at the options first makes it obvious that there is no need to calculate exact values- only in powers of 10. This makes your life a lot easier. If you hadn't noticed this, you might have spent well over 90 seconds trying to calculate the exact value when it wasn't even being asked for.

In other cases, you may actually be able to use the options to arrive at the solution quicker than if you had tried to solve the question as you normally would. Consider the example below:

A region is defined by the two inequalities: $x - y^2 > 1$ *and* $xy > 1$. Which of the following points is in the defined region?

A. (10,3)
B. (10,2)
C. (-10,3)
D. (-10,2)
E. (-10,-3)

Whilst it's possible to solve this question both algebraically or graphically by manipulating the identities, by far **the quickest way is to actually use the options**. Note that options C, D and E violate the second inequality, narrowing down to answer to either A or B. For A: $10 - 3^2 = 1$ and thus this point is on the boundary of the defined region and not actually in the region. Thus, the answer is B (as $10-4 = 6 > 1$.)

In general, it pays dividends to look at the options briefly and see if they can be help you arrive at the question more quickly. Get into this habit early – it may feel unnatural at first but it's guaranteed to save you time in the long run.

Keywords

If you're stuck on a question; pay particular attention to the options that contain key modifiers like "**always**", "**only**", "**all**" as examiners like using them to test if there are any gaps in your knowledge. E.g. the statement "arteries carry oxygenated blood" would normally be true; "All arteries carry oxygenated blood" would be false because the pulmonary artery carries deoxygenated blood.

Section 1

This is the first section of the ECAA and as you walk in, it is inevitable that you will feel nervous. Make sure that you have been to the toilet because once it starts you cannot simply pause and go. Take a few deep breaths and calm yourself down. Remember that panicking will not help and may negatively affect your marks- so try and avoid this as much as possible.

You have one hour to answer 40 questions in section 1. Whilst this section of the ECAA is renowned for being difficult to prepare for, there are powerful shortcuts and techniques that you can use to save valuable time on these types of questions.

You have one and a half minutes per question; this may sound like a lot but it can often not be enough. Some questions in this section are very tricky and can be a big drain on your limited time. **The people who fail to complete section 1 are those who get bogged down on a particular question**.

Therefore, it is vital that you start to get a feel for which questions are going to be easy and quick to do and which ones should be left till the end. The best way to do this is through practice and the questions in this book will offer extensive opportunities for you to do so.

Section 1A

Mathematics

Section 1 mathematics questions are arguably the hardest to prepare for. However, there are some useful techniques you can employ to solve some types of questions much more quickly:

Construct Equations

Some of the problems in Section 1 are quite complex and you'll need to be comfortable with turning prose into equations and manipulating them. For example, when you read "Mark is twice as old as Jon" – this should immediately register as M = 2J. Once you get comfortable forming equations, you can start to approach some of the harder questions in this book (and past papers) which may require you to form and solve simultaneous equations. Consider the example:

Nick has a sleigh that contains toy horses and clowns and counts 44 heads and 132 legs in his sleigh. Given that horses have one head and four legs, and clowns have one head and two legs, calculate the difference between the number of horses and clowns.

   A. 0
   B. 5
   C. 22
   D. 28
   E. 132
   F. More information is needed.
      To start with, let C= Clowns and H= Horses.
      For Heads: $C + H = 44$; For Legs: $2C + 4H = 132$

This now sets up your two equations that you can solve simultaneously.

$C = 44 - H$ so $2(44 - H) + 4H = 132$
Thus, $88 - 2H + 4H = 132$;
Therefore, $2H = 44$; $H = 22$
Substitute back in to give $C = 44 - H = 44 - 22 = 22$
Thus, the difference between horses and clowns $= C - H = 22 - 22 = 0$

It's important you are able to do these types of questions quickly (and **without resorting to trial & error** as they are commonplace in section 1.

Diagrams

When a question asks about timetables, orders or sequences, draw out diagrams. By doing this, you can organise your thoughts and help make sense of the question.

"Mordor is West of Gondor but East of Rivendale. Lorien is midway between Gondor and Mordor. Erebus is West of Mordor. Eden is not East of Gondor."

*Which of the following **cannot** be concluded?*

- **A.** Lorien is East of Erebus and Mordor.
- **B.** Mordor is West of Gondor and East of Erebus.
- **C.** Rivendale is west of Lorien and Gondor.
- **D.** Gondor is East of Mordor and East of Lorien
- **E.** Erebus is West of Mordor and West of Rivendale.

Whilst it is possible to solve this in your head, it becomes much more manageable if you draw a quick diagram and plot the positions of each town:

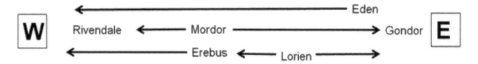

Now, it's a simple case of going through each option and seeing if it is correct according to the diagram. You can now easily see that Option E- Erebus cannot be west of Rivendale.

Don't feel that you have to restrict yourself to linear diagrams like this either – for some questions you may need to draw tables or even Venn diagrams. Consider the example:

Slifers and Osiris are not legendary. Krakens and Minotaurs are legendary. Minotaurs and Lords are both divine. Humans are neither legendary nor divine.

- **A.** Krakens may be only legendary or legendary and divine.
- **B.** Humans are not divine.
- **C.** Slifers are only divine.
- **D.** Osiris may be divine.
- **E.** Humans and Slifers are the same in terms of both qualities.

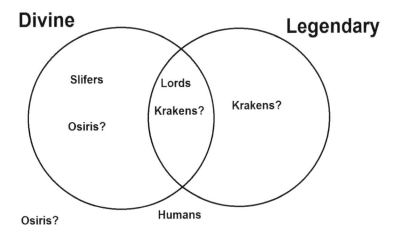

Constructing a Venn diagram allows us to quickly see that the position of Osiris and Krakens aren't certain. Thus, A and D must be true. Humans are neither so B is true. Krakens may be divine so A is true. E cannot be concluded as Slifers are divine but are humans are not. Thus, E is False.

Spatial Reasoning

There are usually 1-2 spatial reasoning questions every year. They usually give nets for a shape or a patterned cuboid and ask which options are possible rotations. Unfortunately, they are extremely difficult to prepare for because the skills necessary to solve these types of questions can take a very long time to improve. The best thing you can do to prepare is to familiarise yourself with the basics of how cube nets work and what the effect of transformations are e.g. what happens if a shape is reflected in a mirror etc.

It is also a good idea to try to learn to draw basic shapes like cubes from multiple angles if you can't do so already. Finally, remember that if the shape is straightforward like a cube, it might be easier for you to draw a net, cut it out and fold it yourself to see which of the options are possible.

If you would like further preparation and training for the maths component of the ECAA, expert classes and support are available through the UniAdmissions ECAA Academy programme. More information can be found here https://www.uniadmissions.co.uk/ecaa-online-course/, alternatively you can call one of our admissions consultants on 44 (0) 800 069 8432

Maths Questions

Question 1:

Robert has a box of building blocks. The box contains 8 yellow blocks and 12 red blocks. He picks three blocks from the box and stacks them up high. Calculate the probability that he stacks two red building blocks and one yellow building block, in **any** order.

A. $\frac{8}{20}$

B. $\frac{44}{95}$

C. $\frac{11}{18}$

D. $\frac{8}{19}$

E. $\frac{12}{20}$

F. $\frac{35}{60}$

Question 2:

Solve $\frac{3x+5}{5} + \frac{2x-2}{3} = 18$

A. 12.11

B. 13.49

C. 13.95

D. 14.2

E. 19

F. 265

Question 3:

Solve $3x^2 + 11x - 20 = 0$

A. $\frac{3}{4}$ and $-\frac{4}{3}$

B. $-\frac{3}{4}$ and $\frac{4}{3}$

C. -5 and $\frac{4}{3}$

D. 5 and $\frac{4}{3}$

E. 12 only

F. -12 only

Question 4:

Express $\frac{5}{x+2} + \frac{3}{x-4}$ as a single fraction.

- A. $\frac{15x-120}{(x+2)(x-4)}$
- B. $\frac{8x-26}{(x+2)(x-4)}$
- C. $\frac{8x-14}{(x+2)(x-4)}$
- D. $\frac{15}{8x}$
- E. 24
- F. $\frac{8x-14}{x^2-8}$

Question 5:

The value of p is directly proportional to the cube root of q. When $p = 12$, $q = 27$. Find q when $p = 24$.
32

- A. 64
- B. 124
- C. 128
- D. 216
- E. 1728

Question 6:

Write 72^2 as a product of its prime factors.

- A. $2^6 \times 3^4$
- B. $2^6 \times 3^5$
- C. $2^4 \times 3^4$
- D. 2×3^3
- E. $2^6 \times 3$
- F. $2^3 \times 3^2$

Question 7:

Calculate: $\frac{2.302 \times 10^5 + 2.302 \times 10^2}{1.151 \times 10^{10}}$

- A. 0.0000202
- B. 0.00020002
- C. 0.00002002
- D. 0.00000002
- E. 0.000002002
- F. 0.000002002

Question 8:

Given that $y^2 + ay + b = (y + 2)^2 - 5$, find the values of **a** and **b**.

	a	b
A	-1	4
B	1	9
C	-1	-9
D	-9	1
E	4	-1
F	4	1

Question 9:

Express $\frac{4}{5} + \frac{m-2n}{m+4n}$ as a single fraction in its simplest form:

   A. $\frac{6m+6n}{5(m+4n)}$

   B. $\frac{9m+26n}{5(m+4n)}$

   C. $\frac{20m+6n}{5(m+4n)}$

   D. $\frac{3m+9n}{5(m+4n)}$

   E. $\frac{3(3m+2n)}{5(m+4n)}$

Question 10:

A is inversely proportional to the square root of B. When A = 4, B = 25.

Calculate the value of A when B = 16.

   A. 0.8
   B. 4
   C. 5
   D. 6
   E. 10
   F. 20

Question 11:

S, T, U and V are points on the circumference of a circle, and O is the centre of the circle.

Given that angle SVU = 89°, calculate the size of the smaller angle SOU.

   A. 89°
   B. 91°
   C. 102°
   D. 178°
   E. 182°

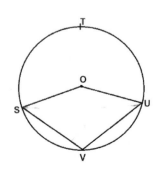

F. $212°$

Question 12:

Open cylinder A has a surface area of 8π cm^2 and a volume of 2π cm^3. Open cylinder B is an enlargement of A and has a surface area of 32π cm^2. Calculate the volume of cylinder B.

A. 2π cm^3
B. 8π cm^3
C. 10π cm^3
D. 14π cm^3
E. 16π cm^3
F. 32π cm^3

Question 13:

Express $\dfrac{8}{x(3-x)} - \dfrac{6}{x}$ in its simplest form.

A. $\dfrac{3x-10}{x(3-x)}$

B. $\dfrac{3x+10}{x(3-x)}$

C. $\dfrac{6x-10}{x(3-2x)}$

D. $\dfrac{6x-10}{x(3+2x)}$

E. $\dfrac{6x-10}{x(3-x)}$

F. $\dfrac{6x+10}{x(3-x)}$

Question 14:

A bag contains 10 balls. 9 of those are white and 1 is black. What is the probability that the black ball is drawn in the tenth and final draw if the drawn balls are not replaced?

A. 0.8
B. $\dfrac{1}{10}$
C. $\dfrac{1}{100}$
D. $\dfrac{1}{10^{10}}$
E. $\dfrac{1}{362,880}$

Question 15:

Gambit has an ordinary deck of 52 cards. What is the probability of Gambit drawing 2 Kings (without replacement)?

A. 0
B. $\dfrac{1}{169}$

C. $\dfrac{1}{221}$

D. $\dfrac{4}{663}$

E. None of the above

Question 16:

I have two identical unfair dice, where the probability that the dice get a 6 is twice as high as the probability of any other outcome, which are all equally likely. What is the probability that when I roll both dice the total will be 12?

    A. 0

    B. $\dfrac{4}{49}$

    C. $\dfrac{1}{9}$

    D. $\dfrac{2}{7}$

    E. None of the above

Question 17:

A roulette wheel consists of 36 numbered spots and 1 zero spot (i.e. 37 spots in total).
What is the probability that the ball will stop in a spot either divisible by 3 or 2?

    A. 0

    B. $\dfrac{25}{37}$

    C. $\dfrac{25}{36}$

    D. $\dfrac{18}{37}$

    E. $\dfrac{24}{37}$

Question 18:

I have a fair coin that I flip 4 times. What is the probability I get 2 heads and 2 tails?

    A. $\dfrac{1}{16}$

    B. $\dfrac{3}{16}$

    C. $\dfrac{3}{8}$

    D. $\dfrac{9}{16}$

    E. None of the above

Question 19:

Shivun rolls two fair dice. What is the probability that he gets a total of 5, 6 or 7?

    A. $\dfrac{9}{36}$

    B. $\dfrac{7}{12}$

C. $\frac{1}{6}$

D. $\frac{5}{12}$

E.

F. None of the above

Question 20:

Dr Savary has a bag that contains x red balls, y blue balls and z green balls (and no others). He pulls out a ball, replaces it, and then pulls out another. What is the probability that he picks one red ball and one green ball?

A. $\frac{2(x+y)}{x+y+z}$

B. $\frac{xz}{(x+y+z)^2}$

C. $\frac{2xz}{(x+y+z)^2}$

D. $\frac{(x+z)}{(x+y+z)^2}$

E. $\frac{4xz}{(x+y+z)^4}$

F. More information needed

Question 21:

Mr Kilbane has a bag that contains x red balls, y blue balls and z green balls (and no others). He pulls out a ball, does **NOT** replace it, and then pulls out another. What is the probability that he picks one red ball and one blue ball?

A. $\frac{2xy}{(x+y+z)^2}$

B. $\frac{2xy}{(x+y+z)(x+y+z-1)}$

C. $\frac{2xy}{(x+y+z)^2}$

D. $\frac{xy}{(x+y+z)(x+y+z-1)}$

E. $\frac{4xy}{(x+y+z-1)^2}$

F. More information needed

Question 22:

There are two tennis players. The first player wins the point with probability p, and the second player wins the point with probability $1 - p$. The rules of tennis say that the first player to score four points wins the game, unless the score is 4-3. At this point the first player to get two points ahead wins.

What is the probability that the first player wins in exactly 5 rounds?

   A. $4p^4(1-p)$

   B. $p^4(1-p)$

   C. $4p(1-p)$

   D. $4p(1-p)^4$

   E. $4p^5(1-p)$

   F. More information needed

Question 23:

Solve the equation $\frac{4x+7}{2} + 9x + 10 = 7$

   A. $\frac{22}{13}$

   B. $-\frac{22}{13}$

   C. $\frac{10}{13}$

   D. $-\frac{10}{13}$

   E. $\frac{13}{22}$

   F. $-\frac{13}{22}$

Question 24:

The volume of a sphere is $V = \frac{4}{3}\pi r^3$, and the surface area of a sphere is $S = 4\pi r^2$. Express S in terms of V

   A. $S = (4\pi)^{2/3}(3V)^{2/3}$

   B. $S = (8\pi)^{1/3}(3V)^{2/3}$

   C. $S = (4\pi)^{1/3}(9V)^{2/3}$

   D. $S = (4\pi)^{1/3}(3V)^{2/3}$

   E. $S = (16\pi)^{1/3}(9V)^{2/3}$

Question 25:

Express the volume of a cube, V, in terms of its surface area, S.

   A. $V = (S/6)^{3/2}$

   B. $V = S^{3/2}$

   C. $V = (6/S)^{3/2}$

   D. $V = (S/6)^{1/2}$

   E. $V = (S/36)^{1/2}$

   F. $V = (S/36)^{3/2}$

Question 26:

Solve the equations $4x + 3y = 7$ and $2x + 8y = 12$

   A. $(x, y) = \left(\frac{17}{13}, \frac{10}{13}\right)$

   B. $(x, y) = \left(\frac{10}{13}, \frac{17}{13}\right)$

   C. $(x, y) = (1, 2)$

   D. $(x, y) = (2, 1)$

   E. $(x, y) = (6, 3)$

   F. $(x, y) = (3, 6)$

   G. No solutions possible.

Question 27:

Rearrange $\frac{(7x+10)}{(9x + 5)} = 3y^2 + 2$, to make x the subject.

   A. $\dfrac{15\,y^2}{7 - 9(3y^2 + 2)}$

   B. $\dfrac{15\,y^2}{7 + 9(3y^2 + 2)}$

   C. $-\dfrac{15\,y^2}{7 - 9(3y^2 + 2)}$

   D. $-\dfrac{15\,y^2}{7 + 9(3y^2 + 2)}$

   E. $-\dfrac{5\,y^2}{7 + 9(3y^2 + 2)}$

   F. $\dfrac{5\,y^2}{7 + 9(3y^2 + 2)}$

Question 28:

Simplify $3x \left(\dfrac{3x^7}{x^{\frac{1}{3}}}\right)^3$

   A. $9x^{20}$

   B. $27x^{20}$

   C. $87x^{20}$

   D. $9x^{21}$

   E. $27x^{21}$

   F. $81x^{21}$

Question 29:

Simplify $2x[(2x)^7]^{\frac{1}{14}}$

   A. $2x\sqrt{2}\,x^4$

   B. $2x\sqrt{2x^3}$

C. $2\sqrt{2\,x^4}$

D. $2\sqrt{2x^3}$

E. $8x^3$

F. $8x$

Question 30:

What is the circumference of a circle with an area of 10π?

A. $2\pi\sqrt{10}$

B. $\pi\sqrt{10}$

C. 10π

D. 20π

E. $\sqrt{10}$

F. More information needed

Question 31:

If $a.b = (ab) + (a+b)$, then calculate the value of $(3.4).5$

A. 19

B. 54

C. 100

D. 119

E. 132

Question 32:

If $a.b = \dfrac{a^b}{a}$, calculate $(2.3).2$

A. $\dfrac{16}{3}$

B. 1

C. 2

D. 4

E. 8

Question 33:

Solve $x^2 + 3x - 5 = 0$

A. $x = -\dfrac{3}{2} \pm \dfrac{\sqrt{11}}{2}$

B. $x = \dfrac{3}{2} \pm \dfrac{\sqrt{11}}{2}$

C. $x = -\dfrac{3}{2} \pm \dfrac{\sqrt{11}}{4}$

D. $x = \dfrac{3}{2} \pm \dfrac{\sqrt{11}}{4}$

E. $x = \frac{3}{2} \pm \frac{\sqrt{29}}{2}$

F. $x = -\frac{3}{2} \pm \frac{\sqrt{29}}{2}$

Question 34:

How many times do the curves $y = x^3$ and $y = x^2 + 4x + 14$ intersect?

A. 0
B. 1
C. 2
D. 3
E. 4

Question 35:

Which of the following graphs **do not** intersect?

1. $y = x$
2. $y = x^2$
3. $y = 1 - x^2$
4. $y = 2$

A. 1 and 2
B. 2 and 3
C. 3 and 4
D. 1 and 3
E. 1 and 4
F. 2 and 4

Question 36:

Calculate the product of 897,653 and 0.009764.

A. 87646.8
B. 8764.68
C. 876.468
D. 87.6468
E. 8.76468
F. 0.876468

Question 37:

Solve for x: $\frac{7x+3}{10} + \frac{3x+1}{7} = 14$

A. $\frac{929}{51}$
B. $\frac{949}{47}$
C. $\frac{949}{79}$

D. $\frac{980}{79}$

Question 38:

What is the area of an equilateral triangle with side length x

A. $\frac{x^2\sqrt{3}}{4}$

B. $\frac{x\sqrt{3}}{4}$

C. $\frac{x^2}{2}$

D. $\frac{x}{2}$

E. x^2

F. x

Question 39:

Simplify $3 - \dfrac{7x(25x^2 - 1)}{49x^2(5x+1)}$

- A. $3 - \dfrac{5x-1}{7x}$
- B. $3 - \dfrac{5x+1}{7x}$
- C. $3 + \dfrac{5x-1}{7x}$
- D. $3 + \dfrac{5x+1}{7x}$
- E. $3 - \dfrac{5x^2}{49}$
- F. $3 + \dfrac{5x^2}{49}$

Question 40:

Solve the equation $x^2 - 10x - 100 = 0$

- A. $-5 \pm 5\sqrt{5}$
- B. $-5 \pm \sqrt{5}$
- C. $5 \pm 5\sqrt{5}$
- D. $5 \pm \sqrt{5}$
- E. $5 \pm 5\sqrt{125}$
- F. $-5 \pm \sqrt{125}$

Question 41:

Rearrange $x^2 - 4x + 7 = y^3 + 2$ to make x the subject.

- A. $x = 2 \pm \sqrt{y^3 + 1}$
- B. $x = 2 \pm \sqrt{y^3 - 1}$
- C. $x = -2 \pm \sqrt{y^3 - 1}$
- D. $x = -2 \pm \sqrt{y^3 + 1}$
- E. x cannot be made the subject for this equation.

Question 42:

Rearrange $3x + 2 = \sqrt{7x^2 + 2x + y}$ to make y the subject.

- A. $y = 4x^2 + 8x + 2$
- B. $y = 4x^2 + 8x + 4$
- C. $y = 2x^2 + 10x + 2$
- D. $y = 2x^2 + 10x + 4$
- E. $y = x^2 + 10x + 2$
- F. $y = x^2 + 10x + 4$

Question 43:

Rearrange $y^4 - 4y^3 + 6y^2 - 4y + 2 = x^5 + 7$ to make y the subject

- A. $y = 1 + (x^5 + 7)^{1/4}$
- B. $y = -1 + (x^5 + 7)^{1/4}$
- C. $y = 1 + (x^5 + 6)^{1/4}$
- D. $y = -1 + (x^5 + 6)^{1/4}$

Question 44:

The aspect ratio of my television screen is 4:3 and the diagonal is 50 inches. What is the area of my television screen?

- A. 1,200 inches^2
- B. 1,000 inches^2
- C. 120 inches^2
- D. 100 inches^2
- E. More information needed.

Question 45:

Rearrange the equation $\sqrt{1 + 3x^{-2}} = y^5 + 1$ to make x the subject.

- A. $x = \dfrac{(y^{10} + 2y^5)}{3}$
- B. $x = \dfrac{3}{(y^{10} + 2y^5)}$
- C. $x = \sqrt{\dfrac{3}{y^{10} + 2y^5}}$
- D. $x = \sqrt{\dfrac{y^{10} + 2y^5}{3}}$
- E. $x = \sqrt{\dfrac{y^{10} + 2y^5 + 2}{3}}$
- F. $x = \sqrt{\dfrac{3}{y^{10} + 2y^5 + 2}}$

Question 46:

Solve $3x - 5y = 10$ and $2x + 2y = 13$.

- A. $(x, y) = (\frac{19}{16}, \frac{85}{16})$
- B. $(x, y) = (\frac{85}{16}, -\frac{19}{16})$
- C. $(x, y) = (\frac{85}{16}, \frac{19}{16})$
- D. $(x, y) = (-\frac{85}{16}, -\frac{19}{16})$
- E. No solutions possible.

Question 47:

A. The two inequalities $x + y \leq 3$ *and* $x^3 - y^2 < 3$ define a region on a plane. Which of the following points is inside the region?

B. (2, 1)

C. (2.5, 1)

D. (1, 2) ✓

E. (3, 5)

F. (1, 2.5)

G. None of the above.

Question 48:

How many times do $y = x + 4$ *and* $y = 4x^2 + 5x + 5$ intersect?

A. 0

B. 1

C. 2

D. 3

E. 4

Question 49:

How many times do $y = x^3$ *and* $y = x$ intersect?

A. 0

B. 1

C. 2

D. 3

E. 4

Question 50:

A cube has unit length sides. What is the length of a line joining a vertex to the midpoint of the opposite side?

A. $\sqrt{2}$

B. $\sqrt{\frac{3}{2}}$

C. $\sqrt{3}$

D. $\sqrt{5}$

E. $\frac{\sqrt{5}}{2}$

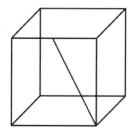

Question 51:

Solve for x, y, and z.

1. $x + y - z = -1$
2. $2x - 2y + 3z = 8$
3. $2x - y + 2z = 9$

	x	y	z
A	2	-15	-14
B	15	2	14
C	14	15	-2
D	-2	15	14
E	2	-15	14
F	No solutions possible		

Question 52:

Fully factorise: $3a^3 - 30a^2 + 75a$

A. $3a(a - 3)^3$
B. $a(3a - 5)^2$
C. $3a(a^2 - 10a + 25)$
D. $3a(a - 5)^2$
E. $3a(a + 5)^2$

Question 53:

Solve for x and y:
$4x + 3y = 48$
$3x + 2y = 34$

	x	y
A	8	6
B	6	8
C	3	4
D	4	3
E	30	12
F	12	30
G	No solutions possible	

Question 54:

Evaluate: $\dfrac{-\left(5^2 - 4 \times 7\right)^2}{-6^2 + 2 \times 7}$

    A. $-\dfrac{3}{50}$

    B. $\dfrac{11}{22}$

    C. $-\dfrac{3}{22}$

    D. $\dfrac{9}{50}$

    E. $\dfrac{9}{22}$

    F. 0

Question 55:

All license plates are 6 characters long. The first 3 characters consist of letters and the next 3 characters of numbers. How many unique license plates are possible?

    A. 676,000

    B. 6,760,000

    C. 67,600,000

    D. 1,757,600

    E. 17,576,000

    F. 175,760,000

Question 56:

How many solutions are there for: $2(2(x^2 - 3x)) = -9$

    A. 0

    B. 1

    C. 2

    D. 3

    E. Infinite solutions

Question 57:

Evaluate: $\left(x^{\frac{1}{2}} y^{-3}\right)^{\frac{1}{2}}$

    A. $\dfrac{x^{\frac{1}{2}}}{y}$

    B. $\dfrac{x}{y^{\frac{3}{2}}}$

    C. $\dfrac{x^{\frac{1}{4}}}{y^{\frac{3}{2}}}$

    D. $\dfrac{y^{\frac{1}{4}}}{x^{\frac{3}{2}}}$

Question 58:

Bryan earned a total of £ 1,240 last week from renting out three flats. From this, he had to pay 10% of the rent from the 1-bedroom flat for repairs, 20% of the rent from the 2-bedroom flat for repairs, and 30% from the 3-bedroom flat for repairs. The 3-bedroom flat costs twice as much as the 1-bedroom flat. Given that the total repair bill was £ 276 calculate the rent for each apartment.

	1 Bedroom	2 Bedrooms	3 Bedrooms
A	280	400	560
B	140	200	280
C	420	600	840
D	250	300	500
E	500	600	1,000

Question 59:

Evaluate: $5\left[5(6^2 - 5 \times 3) + 400^{\frac{1}{2}}\right]^{1/3} + 7$

- A. 0
- B. 25
- C. 32
- D. 49
- E. 56
- F. 200

Question 60:

What is the area of a regular hexagon with side length 1?

- A. $3\sqrt{3}$
- B. $\frac{3\sqrt{3}}{2}$
- C. $\sqrt{3}$
- D. $\frac{\sqrt{3}}{2}$
- E. 6
- F. More information needed

Question 61:

Dexter moves into a new rectangular room that is 19 metres longer than it is wide, and its total area is 780 square metres. What are the room's dimensions?

- A. Width = 20 m; Length = -39 m
- B. Width = 20 m; Length = 39 m
- C. Width = 39 m; Length = 20 m
- D. Width = -39 m; Length = 20 m
- E. Width = -20 m; Length = 39 m

Question 62:

Tom uses 34 meters of fencing to enclose his rectangular lot. He measured the diagonals to 13 metres long. What is the length and width of the lot?

A. 3 m by 4 m
B. 5 m by 12 m
C. 6 m by 12 m
D. 8 m by 15 m
E. 9 m by 15 m
F. 10 m by 10 m

Question 63:

Solve $\frac{3x-5}{2} + \frac{x+5}{4} = x + 1$

A. 1
B. 1.5
C. 3
D. 3.5
E. 4.5
F. None of the above

Question 64:

Calculate: $\frac{5.226 \times 10^6 + 5.226 \times 10^5}{1.742 \times 10^{10}}$

A. 0.033
B. 0.0033
C. 0.00033
D. 0.000033
E. 0.0000033

Question 65:

Calculate the area of the triangle shown to the right:

A. $3 + \sqrt{2}$
B. $\frac{2 + 2\sqrt{2}}{2}$
C. $2 + 5\sqrt{2}$
D. $3 - \sqrt{2}$
E. 3
F. 6

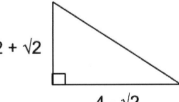

$2 + \sqrt{2}$

$4 - \sqrt{2}$

Question 66:

Rearrange $\sqrt{\dfrac{4}{x} + 9} = y - 2$ to make x the subject.

   A. $x = \dfrac{11}{(y-2)^2}$

   B. $x = \dfrac{9}{(y-2)^2}$

   C. $x = \dfrac{4}{(y+1)(y-5)}$

   D. $x = \dfrac{4}{(y-1)(y+5)}$

   E. $x = \dfrac{4}{(y+1)(y+5)}$

   F. $x = \dfrac{4}{(y-1)(y-5)}$

Question 67:

When 5 is subtracted from 5x the result is half the sum of 2 and 6x. What is the value of x?

   A. 0

   B. 1

   C. 2

   D. 3

   E. 4

   F. 6

Question 68:

Estimate $\dfrac{54.98 + 2.25^2}{\sqrt{905}}$

   A. 0

   B. 1

   C. 2

   D. 3

   E. 4

   F. 5

Question 69:

At a Pizza Parlour, you can order single, double or triple cheese in the crust. You also have the option to include ham, olives, pepperoni, bell pepper, meat balls, tomato slices, and pineapples. How many different types of pizza are available at the Pizza Parlour?

   A. 10

   B. 96

   C. 192

   D. 384

   E. 768

   F. None of the above

Question 70:

Solve the simultaneous equations $x^2 + y^2 = 1$ and $x + y = \sqrt{2}$, for x, y > 0

- A. $(x, y) = (\frac{\sqrt{2}}{2}, \frac{\sqrt{2}}{2})$
- B. $(x, y) = (½, \frac{\sqrt{3}}{2})$
- C. $(x, y) = (\sqrt{2} - 1, 1)$
- D. $(x, y) = (\sqrt{2}, ½)$

Question 71:

How many negative roots does $f(x) = 16x^4 + 32x^3 + 24x^2 + 8x + 1$ have?

- A. 0
- B. 1
- C. 2
- D. 3
- E. 4
- F. 5

Question 72:

Solve the inequality $x^2 \geq 6 - x$

- A. $x \leq -3$ and $x \leq 2$
- B. $x \leq -3$ and $x \geq 2$
- C. $x \geq -3$ and $x \leq 2$
- D. $x \geq -3$ and $x \geq 2$
- E. $x \geq 2$ only
- F. $x \geq -3$ only

Question 73:

The hypotenuse of an equilateral right-angled triangle is x cm. What is the area of the triangle in terms of x?

- A. $\frac{\sqrt{x}}{2}$
- B. $\frac{x^2}{4}$
- C. $\frac{x}{4}$
- D. $\frac{3x^2}{4}$
- E. $\frac{x^2}{10}$

Question 74:

Mr Heard derives a formula: $Q = \frac{(X+Y)^2 A}{3B}$. He doubles the values of X and Y, halves the value of A and triples the value of B. What happens to value of Q?

    A. Decreases by $\frac{1}{3}$

    B. Increases by $\frac{1}{3}$

    C. Decreases by $\frac{2}{3}$

    D. Increases by $\frac{2}{3}$

    E. Increases by $\frac{4}{3}$

    F. Decreases by $\frac{4}{3}$

Question 75:

Consider the graphs $y = x^2 - 2x + 3$, and $y = x^2 - 6x - 10$. Which of the following is true?

    A. Both equations intersect the x-axis.
    B. Neither equation intersects the x-axis.
    C. The first equation does not intersect the x-axis; the second equation intersects the x-axis.
    D. The first equation intersects the x-axis; the second equation does not intersect the x-axis.

Question 76:

A crocodile's tail weighs 30kg. Its head weighs as much as the tail and one half of the body and legs. The body and legs together weigh as much as the tail and head combined. What is the total weight of the crocodile?

    A. 220kg
    B. 240kg
    C. 260kg
    D. 280kg
    E. 300kg

Question 77:

Evaluate the following: $\frac{4.2 \times 10^{10} - 4.2 \times 10^6}{2 \times 10^3}$

    A. 2.09979 x 106
    B. 2.09979 x 107
    C. 2.09979 x 108
    D. 2.09979 x 109
    E. 2.09979 x 1010

Question 78:

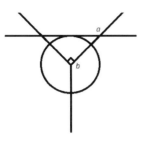

A. Calculate a – b

B. 0°

C. 5°

D. 10°

E. 15°

F. 20°

Question 79:

Jack has a bag with a complete set of snooker balls (15 red, 1 yellow, 1 green, 1 brown, 1 blue, 1 pink and 1 black ball) within it. Blindfolded Jack draws two balls from the bag.

What is the probability that he draws a blue and a black ball in any order?

A. 2/41

B. 1/210

C. 2/210

D. 1/105

E. 2/441

Question 80:

Which is the equivalent function to: $y = 9x^{-\frac{1}{3}}$

A. $y = \dfrac{1}{x}$

B. $y = \sqrt[3]{9x}$

C. $y = \dfrac{1}{\sqrt[3]{9x}}$

D. $y = \dfrac{9}{\sqrt[3]{x}}$

E. $y = \dfrac{3}{\sqrt[3]{x}}$

Question 81:

Make y the subject of the formula: $\dfrac{y+x}{x} = \dfrac{x}{a} + \dfrac{a}{x}$

A. $y = \dfrac{x^2}{a} + a$

B. $y = \dfrac{x^2+a^2-ax}{a}$

C. $y = \dfrac{-ax}{x^2+a^2}$

D. $y = \dfrac{x^2}{ax} + a - x$

E. $y = a^2 - ax$

Question 82:

The graph below shows a circle with radius 5 and centre (0,0).

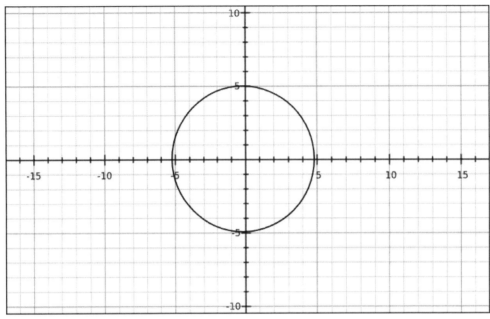

What are the values of x when the line $y = 3x - 5$ meets the circle?

    A. $x = 0$ or $x = 3$
    B. $x = 0$ or $x = 3.5$
    C. $x = 1$ or $x = 3.5$
    D. $x = 1.5$ or $x = -3$
    E. $x = 1.5$ or $x = -2$

Question 83:

There are 1000 international airports in the world. If 4 flights take off every hour from each airport, estimate the annual number of commercial flights worldwide, to the nearest 1 million

    A.   20 million
    B.   35 million
    C.   37 million
    D.   40 million
    E.   42 million
    F.   44 million

Question 84:

How many seconds are there in 66 weeks? $[n! = 1 \times 2 \times 3 \times ... \times n]$

- A. 7!
- B. 8!
- C. 9!
- D. 10!
- E. 11!
- F. 12!

Question 85:

Write $\frac{\sqrt{20}-2}{\sqrt{5}+3}$ in the form: $p\sqrt{5} + q$

$2\sqrt{5} - 4$

$3\sqrt{5} - 4$

$3\sqrt{5} - 5$

$4\sqrt{5} - 6$

$5\sqrt{5} + 4$

Question 86:

Consider the triangle right where BE = 4cm, EC = 2cm and AC = 9cm. What is the length of side DE?

- A. 4cm
- B. 5.5cm
- C. 6cm
- D. 7.5cm
- E. 8cm

Question 87:

An investment of £500 is made in a compound interest account. At the end of 3 years the balance reads £1687.50. What is the interest rate?

- A. 20%
- B. 35%
- C. 50%
- D. 65%
- E. 80%

Question 88:

Rupert plays one game of tennis and one game of squash.
The probability that he will win the tennis game is 3/4

The probability that he will win the squash game is 1/3
What is the probability that he will win one game only?

    A. 3/12
    B. 7/12
    C. 4/5
    D. 13/12
    E. 7/6

Question 89:

Calculate the perimeter of a regular polygon each interior angle is 150o and each side is 15 cm.

    A. 75 cm
    B. 150 cm
    C. 180 cm
    D. 225 cm
    E. 1,500 cm
    F. More information is needed.

Question 90:

Calculate $\dfrac{1.25 \times 10^{10} + 1.25 \times 10^{9}}{2.5 \times 10^{8}}$

    A. 0
    B. 1
    C. 55
    D. 110
    E. 1.25×10^{8}
    F. 5.5×10^{7}
    G. 5.5×10^{8}

Question 91:

Solve $y = 2x - 1$ and $y = x^{2} - 1$ for x and y

    A. $(0, -1)$ and $(2, 3)$
    B. $(1, -1)$ and $(2, 2)$
    C. $(1, 4)$ and $(3, 2)$
    D. $(2, -3)$ and $(4, 5)$
    E. $(3, -1)$ and $(3, 1)$
    F. $(4, -2)$ and $(-2, 4)$

Question 92:

Simplify fully: $\dfrac{(3x^{½})^{3}}{3x^{2}}$

    A. $\dfrac{3x}{\sqrt{x}}$
    B. $\dfrac{9}{x}$

C. $3x^{\frac{1}{2}}$

D. $3x\sqrt{x}$

E. $\frac{9}{\sqrt{x}}$

Question 93:

Study the diagram, comprising regular pentagons. What is the product of a and b?

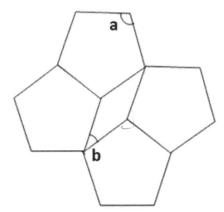

A. 580°

B. 1,111°

C. 3,888°

D. 7,420°

E. 9,255°

F. 15552°

Question 94:

Tim stands at the waterfront and holds a 30 cm ruler horizontally at eye level one metre in front of him. It lines up so it appears to be exactly the same length as a cruise ship 1 km out to sea. How long is the cruise ship?

A. 299.7 m

B. 300.0 m

C. 333.3 m

D. 29,970 m

E. 30,000 m

Question 95:

Bob is twice as old as Kerry, and Kerry is three times as old as Bob's son. Their ages combined make 50 years. How old was Bob when his son was born?

A. 15

B. 20

C. 25

D. 30

E. 35

Question 96:

The mean of a set of 11 numbers is 6. Two numbers are removed, and the mean is now 5. Which of the following is not a possible combination of removed numbers?

A. 1 and 20

B. 6 and 9

C. 10 and 11

D. 15 and 6

E. 19 and 2

Question 97:

Evaluate: $\dfrac{3.4 \; x \; 10^{11} + 3.4 \; x \; 10^{10}}{6.8 \; x \; 10^{12}}$

    A. $5.5 \; x \; 10^{-12}$
    B. $5.5 \; x \; 10^{-2}$
    C. $5.5 \; x \; 10^{1}$
    D. $5.5 \; x \; 10^{2}$
    E. $5.5 \; x \; 10^{10}$
    F. $5.5 \; x \; 10^{12}$

Question 98:

A circle has a radius of 3 metres. A line passes through the circle's centre and intersects with a tangent 4 metres from its tangent point. How far is this point of intersection from the centre of the circle?

    A. 1 metre
    B. 3 metres
    C. 5 metres
    D. 7 metres
    E. 9 metres

Question 99:

Consider the equations: A: $y = 3x$ and B: $y = \dfrac{6}{x} - 7$. At what values of x do the two equations intersect?

    A. $x = 2$ and $x = 9$
    B. $x = 3$ and $x = 6$
    C. $x = 6$ and $x = 27$
    D. $x = 6$
    E. $x = 18$

Question 100:

Calculate the radius of a sphere which has a surface area three times as great as its volume.

    A. 0.5
    B. 1
    C. 1.5
    D. 2
    E. 2.5
    F. More information is needed

Question 101:

The diagram shows a series of identical sports fields, calculate the shortest distance between points A and B.

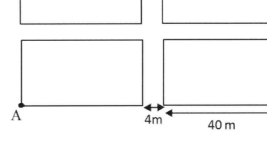

A. 100 m
B. 105 m
C. 146 m
D. 148 m
E. 154 m
F. None of the above.

Question 102:

Simplify fully: $1 + \left(3\sqrt{2} - 1\right)^2 + \left(3 + \sqrt{2}\right)^2$

A. $30 + 6\sqrt{2} - 2\sqrt{18}$
B. $30 + 6\sqrt{2} + 2\sqrt{18}$
C. $3\left[2\left(\sqrt{2} - 1\right) + 2\right]$
D. 24
E. 29
F. 31

Question 103:

Each vertex of a square lies directly on the edge of a circle with a radius of 1cm. Calculate the area of the circle that is not occupied by the square. Use $\pi = 3$.

A. 0.25cm^2
B. 0.5cm^2
C. 0.75cm^2
D. 1.0cm^2
E. 1.25cm^2
F. 1.5cm^2

Question 104:

If $(3p + 5)^2 = 24p + 49$, calculate p

A. -5 or -9
B. -3 or -6
C. -4 or 6
D. -6 or 4
E. 4 or -2

Question 105:

Find the values of angles b and c.

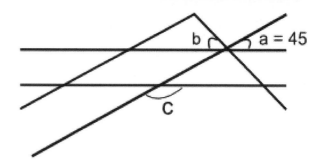

- **A.** 45° and 135°
- **B.** 45° and 130°
- **C.** 50° and 135°
- **D.** 55° and 130°
- **E.** More information needed.

Question 106:

If the lines $y_1 = (n + 1)x + 10$ and $y_2 = (n + 3)x + 2$ are perpendicular, then n must equal which of the following?

- **A.** 2
- **B.** -2
- **C.** 3
- **D.** -3
- **E.** 0
- **F.** 1

Question 107:

A formula: $\sqrt[3]{\frac{z(x+y)(1+m-n)}{3}}$ is given. Would you expect this formula to calculate?

- **A.** A length
- **B.** An area
- **C.** A volume
- **D.** A volume of rotation
- **E.** A geometric average

Question 108:

What is the equation of the line of best fit for the scatter graph below?

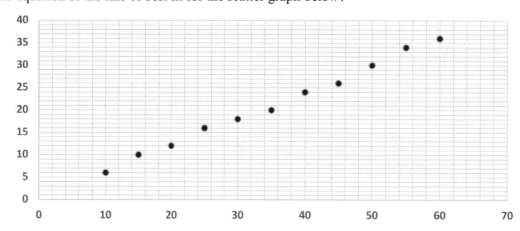

- **A.** $y = 0.2x + 0.35$
- **B.** $y = 0.2x - 0.35$

C. $y = 0.4x + 0.35$
D. $y = 0.4x - 0.35$
E. $y = 0.6x + 0.35$

Question 109:

What is the median of the following numbers: $\frac{7}{36}$; $0.\dot{3}$; $\frac{11}{18}$; 0.25; 0.75; $\frac{62}{72}$; $\frac{7}{7}$

A. $\frac{7}{36}$

B. $0.\dot{3}$

C. $\frac{11}{18}$

D. $\frac{62}{72}$

E. 0.75

Question 110:

The table below shows the results of a study investigating antibiotic resistance in staphylococcus populations.

Antibiotic	Number of Bacteria tested	Number of Resistant Bacteria
Benzyl-penicillin	1011	98
Chloramphenicol	109	1200
Metronidazole	108	256
Erythtomycin	105	2

A single staphylococcus bacterium is chosen at random from a similar population. Resistance to any one antibiotic is independent of resistance to others. Calculate the probability that the bacterium selected will be resistant to all four drugs.

A. 1 in 1012
B. 1 in 106
C. 1 in 1020
D. 1 in 1025
E. 1 in 1030
F. 1 in 1035

Question 111:

Solve $y = x^2 - 3x + 4$ and $y - x = 1$ as (x, y).

A. $(-1, 2)$ and $(3, 4)$
B. $(1, 2)$ and $(3, 4)$
C. $(7, -2)$ and $(6, 5)$
D. $(2, -3)$ and $(4, -1)$
E. $(1, -1)$ and $(-7, -1)$

Question 112:

Evaluate the following expression:

$$\left(\left(\frac{6}{8}\times\frac{7}{3}\right) \div \left(\frac{7}{5}\times\frac{2}{6}\right)\right) \times 0.40 \times 15\% \times 5\% \times \pi \times \left(\sqrt{e^2}\right) \times 0.20 \times (e\pi)^{-1}$$

    A. $\frac{4}{55}$

    B. $\frac{8}{770}$

    C. $\frac{9}{4,000}$

    D. $\frac{8}{54,321}$

    E. $\frac{9}{67,800}$

Question 113:

Bill wants to lay down laminate flooring in his living room, which has an in-built circular fish tank that he will have to lay the flooring around. He has decided to buy planks that he can cut to fit the dimensions of his room. He must, however, buy whole planks and cut them down himself. The room's dimensions are given below, as are those of one plank.

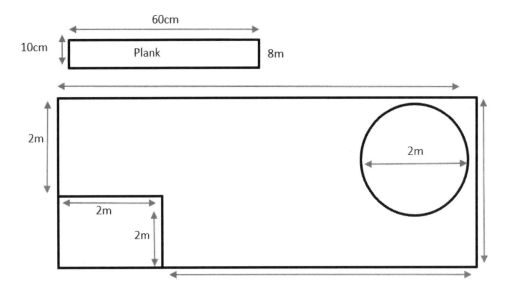

Calculate the number of planks needed to cover the whole floor. Take $\pi = 3$.

    A. 30

    B. 417

    C. 600

    D. 589

    E. 43

Question 114:

Rearrange $\frac{(16x+11)}{(4x+5)} = 4y^2 + 2$ to make x the subject

A. $x = \dfrac{20y^2-1}{[16-4\,(4y^2+2)]}$

B. $x = \dfrac{20y^2-8}{[16-6\,(4y^2+2)]}$

C. $x = \dfrac{6y^2-1}{[16-4\,(4y^2+2)]}$

D. $x = \dfrac{21y^2-1}{[16-4\,(2y^2+2)]}$

E. $x = \dfrac{7y^2-1}{[6-14\,(6+7)]}$

Question 115:

How many positive roots does the function $f(x) = x^4 - 8x^3 + 22x^2 - 24x$ have?

A. 0

B. 1

C. 2

D. 3

E. None of the above

Question 116:

Compute the integral $\int_0^1 \frac{x-4}{\sqrt{x}(\sqrt{x}+2)}\,dx$

A. -3

B. -1

C. 2

D. 3

E. 1

Question 117:

Given that, in the expansion of $(3x + b)^7$, the coefficient of x^4 is the same as the coefficient of x^2 in $(3b + x)^4$, find b.

A. $\dfrac{2}{105}$

B. $\dfrac{105}{2}$

C. $\dfrac{107}{3}$

D. $\dfrac{3}{107}$

E. $\dfrac{109}{4}$

Question 118:

Consider the tangent to the curve $y = x^2 + bx$. For what values of b is the x intercept greater than 4?

    A. $-3 < b < 3$

    B. $2 < b < 4$

    C. $b > 3$

    D. $b < -3$

    E. $b > -3$

Question 119:

Given $f(x) = \left(9x^2 + 12 + \frac{4}{x^2}\right)^{\frac{1}{2}}$ and $\frac{d^n f}{dx^n}(2) = -\frac{3}{4}$ find n.

    A. 1

    B. 2

    C. 3

    D. 4

    E. 5

Question 120:

In which of the following ranges is $(x^2 - 1)(x + 2)(x + 4) > 0$?

    A. $-2 < x < 1$

    B. $-1 < x < 2$

    C. $-2 < x < -1$

    D. $x \geq 1$

    E. $x < -3$

Question 121:

Suppose $5^{4+6+\cdots+2x} = 0.04^{-14}$. Given x is a positive integer, what is x?

    A. 5

    B. 6

    C. 7

    D. 8

    E. 5.5

Question 122:

Four unbiased coins are tossed. What is the probability of getting at most two heads?

    A. $\frac{3}{4}$

    B. $\frac{7}{8}$

    C. $\frac{5}{6}$

D. $\dfrac{1}{2}$

E. $\dfrac{2}{3}$

Question 123:

An arithmetic series is defined by

$$x_1 = 2$$

$$x_{n+1} = x_n + q$$

Given x_{100} is 13, find the sum to infinity of a series with common ratio q, and first term 5

A. $\dfrac{78}{5}$

B. $\dfrac{102}{3}$

C. $\dfrac{36}{7}$

D. $\dfrac{52}{9}$

E. $\dfrac{45}{8}$

Question 124:

The roots of $x^2 + 3x + c = 2$ differ by 7. What is c?

A. -10

B. -8

C. 13

D. -4

E. 5

Question 125:

Which of the following is a line of symettry of the graph $y = \dfrac{1}{\sin(4x+\frac{\pi}{3})}$

A. $x = \dfrac{13\pi}{2}$

B. $x = \dfrac{pi}{2}$

C. $x = \pi$

D. $x = \dfrac{13\pi}{24}$

E. $y = \dfrac{\pi}{24}$

Question 126:

Define a recurrent sequence by $x_{n+1} = \begin{cases} \frac{x_n}{2} & \text{if } x_n \text{ even} \\ 3x_n + 1 & \text{if } x_n \text{ odd} \end{cases}$

Given $x_1 = 12$, what is x_{100}?

A. 1
B. 4
C. 2
D. 12
E. 0

Question 127:

What is the sum of roots of the equation $2^y - 5\sqrt{2}^{y+2} + 24 = 0$

A. $3 + 4\log_2 5$
B. 4
C. 10
D. $\log_2 24$
E. $6 + 2\log_2 3$

Question 128:

For $p > 0$, find the area enclosed by the curves $y = px^2$ and $x = py^2$

A. $\dfrac{1}{3p}$
B. $3p$
C. $\dfrac{1}{3p^2}$
D. $\dfrac{1}{2}p^2$
E. $3p$

Question 129:

What is the complete set of values for which $\dfrac{x^2+2x}{\sqrt{x^3}}$ is increasing?

A. $x > 3$
B. $x < 2$
C. $2 < x < 4$
D. $x > 2$
E. $0 < x < 2$

Question 130:

What is the probability of rolling the same number exactly three times with five six-sided dice?

A. $\dfrac{10}{36}$

B. $\dfrac{17}{32}$

C. $\dfrac{125}{648}$

D. $\dfrac{108}{124}$

E. $\dfrac{133}{648}$

Question 131:

Compute the shortest distance between the curves

$x^2 + 4x + y^2 + 6y + 10 = 0$ and $x^2 - 4x + y^2 - 8y + 12 = 0$

   A. $\sqrt{65} - \sqrt{2} - \sqrt{3}$

   B. $\sqrt{65} - 2\sqrt{2} - 2\sqrt{3}$

   C. $\sqrt{65} - 2\sqrt{2} - \sqrt{3}$

   D. $\sqrt{65}$

   E. $\sqrt{65} - 4\sqrt{2} - 2\sqrt{3}$

Question 132:

How many solutions does the equation $\cos 2x \log x = \sin 2x$ have in range $0 < x < 3\pi$

   A. 0

   B. 3

   C. 5

   D. 6

   E. 7

Question 133:

The sum to infinity of a geometric progression is 4. The sum to infinity of the squares of each term in the progression is 10. What is the common ratio of the geometric series?

   A. $\dfrac{1}{2}$

   B. $\dfrac{2}{5}$

   C. $\dfrac{3}{7}$

   D. $\dfrac{7}{12}$

   E. $\dfrac{3}{13}$

Question 134:

Given that $\dfrac{dV}{dt} = (1 + t)^4$, and $V(1) = 5$, what is $V(2)$?

   A. $\dfrac{174}{5}$

B. $\dfrac{236}{5}$

C. $\dfrac{112}{3}$

D. $\dfrac{89}{4}$

Question 135:

The sum of the first n terms of an arithmetic series is S_n. For a particular series, $S_3 = 18$ and the fifth term is k. Which of the following are necessary conditions on k for S_n to be an integer for every value of n?

    I. k has a factor of 6

    II. k has a factor of 18

    III. k is odd

    A. None

    B. I only

    C. II only

    D. III only

    E. I & II only

    F. I & III only

    G. II & III only

    H. All three

Question 136:

When is $\dfrac{\sin 2x}{1-\cos 2x}(3^x - 2) \le 0$ in the range $0 < x < \pi$?

    A. $\log_3 2 \le x \le \dfrac{\pi}{2}$

    B. $\log_3 2 \le x < \dfrac{\pi}{2}$

    C. $\dfrac{\pi}{2} < x \le \log_3 2$

    D. $0 < x < \log_3 2$

    E. $\dfrac{\pi}{2} \le x \le \log_3 2$

    F. $0 < x \le \log_3 2$

Question 137:

What is the difference between the 2 solutions to the equation $25^{x-1} + \dfrac{96}{25} = 5^x$?

    A. $\log_5 \dfrac{3}{2}$

    B. 25

    C. 5

    D. 1

    E. $\log_5 \dfrac{5}{3}$

Question 138:

What is the equation of the line equidistant between the centres of the circles $y^2 + x^2 + 6y - 4x + 12 = 0$ and $y^2 + x^2 - 2y - 80 = 0$?

   A. $y = 1 - 2x$

   B. $y = \frac{x-3}{2}$

   C. $y = \frac{1}{2} - 2x$

   D. $y = -x$

   E. $y = \frac{x}{2} + 1$

Question 139:

A small marble is carried from point A, to point B, and then to point C, which have co-ordinates $(4, 6, 12)$, $(7, 2, 0)$ and $(16, 15, 5)$ respectively.

   What is the difference between the square of the distance the marble travelled and the square of the distance it is currently from where it started?

   A. 170

   B. $10(17 + 13\sqrt{11})$

   C. 30

   D. $10(17 - 13\sqrt{11})$

   E. $3\sqrt{61} + 130\sqrt{11}$

Question 140:

Find the distance between the stationary points of $y = 5x^3 - 5x + 6 = 0$.

   A. $\frac{2\sqrt{109}}{3\sqrt{3}}$

   B. $\frac{2\sqrt{34}}{3\sqrt{3}}$

   C. There is 1 or fewer stationary points.

   D. $\frac{2}{3}$

   E. $\sqrt{34}$

Question 141:

What is the digit in the 10,000s place in the number 301^5?

   A. 0

   B. 9

   C. 3

   D. 5

   E. 1

   F. 2

   G. 7

Question 142:

Consider the sequence defined by

$x_1 = 1000$

$$x_{n+1} = \frac{1}{\sqrt{x_n}} \quad n \geq 0$$

What is x_{1000}?

    A. $10^{3 \times 2^{1000}}$

    B. $10^{-3 \times 2^{-1000}}$

    C. $10^{3 \times 2^{999}}$

    D. $10^{-3 \times 2^{-999}}$

    E. $10^{-3 \times 2^{-1001}}$

    F. $10^{3 \times 2^{-999}}$

    G. $10^{-3 \times 2^{100}}$

Question 143:

$4x^2 - 7x + 1$ is multiplied by $2x - q$ to form $f(x)$.

$f(x)$ divided by $(x + 2)$ is -31^2.

    What is q?

    A. 27

    B. 35

    C. There is no such q.

    D. -27

    E. -35

    F. $\frac{21}{2}$

Question 144:

What is the value of the integral below?

$$\int_0^2 |x - 1|\left(3\sqrt{x} - x\sqrt{x}\right)dx$$

    A. $\frac{48 - 4\sqrt{2}}{35}$

    B. $\frac{4\sqrt{2}}{35}$

    C. $\frac{24}{35}$

D. $\frac{48+4\sqrt{2}}{35}$

E. $\frac{24+4\sqrt{2}}{35}$

F. $\frac{24-4\sqrt{2}}{35}$

Question 145:

For a function $f(x)$, it is given that $\left(\int_0^2 f(x)dx\right)\left(\int_0^1 f(x)dx + 4\right)=24$. You are also told that, for this function, $f(x-1) = f(1-x)$.

Which of the following could the value of $\int_1^2 f(x)dx$ be?

I. -6
II. 8
III. 2

A. None
B. I only
C. II only
D. III only
E. I & II only
F. I & III only
G. II & III only
H. All three

Question 146:

Calculate the value of $\sqrt{20 - 20\sqrt{5} + 25} + \sqrt{5 - 8\sqrt{5} + 16}$.

A. $9 - 3\sqrt{5}$
B. $1-\sqrt{5}$
C. $\sqrt{5} - 1$
D. $3\sqrt{5} - 9$
E. $\sqrt{66 - 28\sqrt{5}}$
F. 13
G. -3

Question 147:

A hospital has two wards, one for critically ill patients called Ward A and one for general patients, called Ward B. The probability a patient in Ward A survives is $\frac{1}{9}$, and the probability a patient in Ward B survives is $\frac{3}{5}$. (Every patient is in one of the two wards).

Given that there are p people in Ward A, and the overall survival rate of the hospital is $\frac{1}{4}$, what is q, the number of people in Ward B, in terms of p?

A. $\dfrac{3p}{45}$

B. $\dfrac{45p}{3}$

C. $\dfrac{25p}{63}$

D. $\dfrac{63p}{25}$

E. 50

F. $\dfrac{45p}{12p-45}$

G. $\dfrac{12p-45}{45p}$

Question 148:

A man tosses a fair coin 7 times. What is P(he gets more than 4 heads and two of the last 3 tosses are heads)?

A. $\dfrac{3}{16}$

B. $\dfrac{7}{8}$

C. $\dfrac{33}{128}$

D. $\dfrac{3}{8}$

E. $\dfrac{33}{64}$

F. $\dfrac{279}{512}$

Question 149:

I have 2 blue balls and 3 red balls which I will throw into 5 indistinguishable boxes. Assuming I don't miss, how many distinct situations could I be in after all the balls are thrown?

A. 14

B. 5^5

C. 32

D. 16

E. 8

F. 4

G. $5^3 + 5^2$

Question 150:

Let $f(x)$ be $\left(\dfrac{x}{2} + 1\right)^3$.

What if the value of $f''(2)$?

A. 3

B. 63

C. 27

D. $\frac{63}{2}$

E. -2

Question 151:

Let $f(x) = ax^3 + bx^2 + cx - 75$ for some integers a, b, c. $f\left(\frac{3}{4}\right) = f(-5) = 0$ and $f(x) = 0$ for only these values. What is the mean of the numbers a, b, c?

 A. 50

 B. -35

 C. $\frac{115}{3}$

 D. 35

 E. $-\frac{43}{3}$

 F. 12

Question 152:

Let $f(x) = ax^5 + \frac{x^4}{2} + cx$. It is given that the gradient of this function at $x = 1$ is $-a^2$. What is the maximum value of $\int_0^2 f(x)dx$?

 A. 67/36

 B. $-\frac{67}{18}$

 C. -67/36

 D. $\frac{67}{18}$

Question 153:

$1, \frac{2}{3}, \& \frac{4}{9}$ are 3 of the first 7 terms of a geometric series. Which of the following are not possible values of the sum to infinity of the series?

 I. $3 + \sqrt{6}$

 II. $\frac{9}{2}$

 III. $\frac{9 + 3\sqrt{6}}{2}$

 IV. $\frac{27}{4}$

  A. I only

  B. II only

  C. III only

  D. IV only

  E. I & III only

  F. II& III only

  G. II & IV only

Question 154:

$\frac{dx}{dt} = 6\left(\frac{1}{1-\sin t} - \frac{1}{1+\sin t}\right)$. If $x = 0$ when $t = \frac{\pi}{6}$, find x when $t = \frac{\pi}{3}$. [the integral of $\frac{1}{\cos^2 t}$ *is* $\tan t$]

- A. $4\sqrt{3}$
- B. $6\sqrt{3}$
- C. $\frac{6}{\sqrt{3}}$
- D. $3\sqrt{3}$
- E. $\sqrt{3}$
- F. $\frac{4}{\sqrt{3}}$
- G. $12\sqrt{3}$

Question 155:

What angle is swept by the minute hand on a clock between 08:34 and 11:12?

- A. $1260°$
- B. $948°$
- C. $924°$
- D. $720°$
- E. $724°$

Question 156:

An inflated spherical football is packaged in the smallest possible box that it will fit inside of. What is the ratio of volume taken up by the football to the volume of the box?

- A. $\frac{\pi}{12} : 1$
- B. $\frac{12}{\pi} : 1$
- C. $\frac{6}{\pi} : 1$
- D. $\frac{\pi}{6} : 1$
- E. $\frac{8}{\pi} : 1$

Question 157:

The diagram below shows a scalene triangle with a line crossing through it parallel to the base. What is the length of the base, which is marked 'x'?

A. $6\frac{1}{7}$ m

B. $7\frac{5}{8}$ m

C. $6\frac{3}{8}$ m

D. $6\frac{6}{7}$ m

E. $7\frac{1}{6}$ m

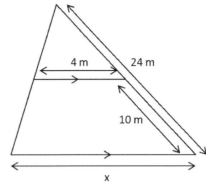

Question 158:

There are five rides in a theme park which are arranged on the corners of a regular pentagon, as shown in the diagram below.

If someone wants to walk from ride 2 to ride 4, what bearing should they walk on?

A. 45°

B. 54°

C. 112°

D. 234°

E. 245°

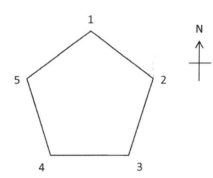

Question 159:

What is the area of the grey section in the diagram below?

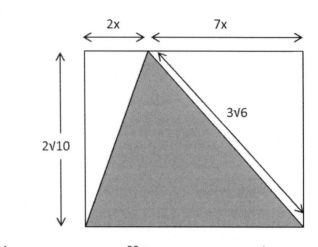

- **A.** $12\sqrt{15}$
- **B.** $18\sqrt{10}$
- **C.** $\frac{18}{7}\sqrt{35}$
- **D.** $\frac{6}{5}\sqrt{15}$
- **E.** $\frac{43}{9}\sqrt{35}$

Question 160:

The diagram shows a garden, the grey area is to be covered with grass. The grass comes in rolls that are 1 m by 10 m. How many rolls are needed to cover the garden?

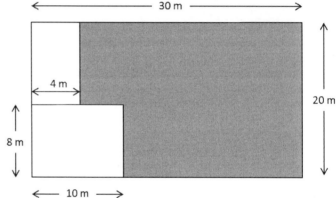

- **A.** 47
- **B.** 48
- **C.** 49
- **D.** 50
- **E.** 51

Question 161:

In a household there are two people with size 6 feet and three people with size 11 feet. Each person owns four pairs of shoes. All of the shoes are randomly mixed up in a large bag. If someone pulls out a left size 11 shoe, what is the probability that the next shoe that they pull out is a right size 11 shoe?

- **A.** 1/2
- **B.** 12/39
- **C.** 3/10
- **D.** 11/39
- **E.** 16/39

Question 162:

What is the surface area to volume ratio of a solid cylinder with radius 'r' and length '3r'?

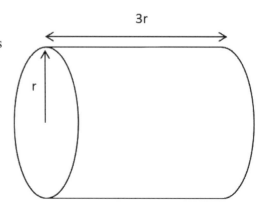

- **A.** $3 : r$
- **B.** $4\frac{1}{3} : r$
- **C.** $8 : 3r$
- **D.** $1 : 6r$
- **E.** $4 : 1r$

Question 163:

Consider the parabola $y = (x - 3)^2 - 4$ and the line $y = mx + c$. Let R be the size of the interval m must lie in such that the line and parabola do not intersect. What is c in terms of R?

   A. $c = 5 - R^2$

   B. $c = 5 - \dfrac{(R+6)^2}{4}$

   C. $c = 5 - \dfrac{R^2}{16}$

   D. $c = 20 - \dfrac{R^2}{4}$

   E. $c = 20 - (R + 6)^2$

Question 164:

Let $f(x) = 3x^5 + 8x^4 + x^3 - 4x - 16 = 0$. You are told that $f(-2) = 0 = f(1)$. How many distinct real roots does $f(x)$ have?

   A. 0

   B. 1

   C. 2

   D. 3

   E. 4

   F. 5

   G. 6

Question 165:

Let a_n be a geometric series with first term a_0 , common difference d, and the sum of the first n terms be S_n. Which of the following conditions is sufficient for the product of any two terms in the series to always be greater than 0, no matter which two terms are chosen?

   I. $S_5 = a_{10}$

   II. $S_5 = a_{12}$

   III. $a_0 = d$

   A. None

   B. I only

   C. II only

   D. III only

   E. I & II only

   F. I & III only

   G. II & III only

   H. All three

Question 166:

The expansion of $(k + x)^5$ has at least two terms with the same coefficient, as does the expansion of $(1 + 2kx)^2$. How many possible values of k are there?

A. 0
B. 1
C. 2
D. 3
E. 4
F. 5

Question 167:

How many solutions are there to $x \times 3^{\tan 2x} = 1$ in the range $0 < x < \pi$?

A. 0
B. 1
C. 2
D. 3
E. 4
F. 5

Question 168:

Find the distance between the intersection points of $y = |x - 4|$ and $y = 5 - |x - 1|$.

A. There are no intersections.
B. 4
C. $\sqrt{34}$
D. 5
E. 3
F. $\sqrt{41}$

Question 169:

Given that $\int_0^4 (x^3 + ax^2 + bx + 1)dx = 0$, and that $a \le 0, b \ge 0$, what is the maximum value of $\int_0^3 (x^3 + ax^2 + bx + 1)dx$?

A. -15
B. 15
C. 100
D. -100
E. $\dfrac{123}{2}$
F. $-\dfrac{123}{2}$

Question 170:

Let $f(x) = \dfrac{\left(x^2 - \frac{1}{x}\right)^2}{x^{\frac{1}{3}}}$. It is given also that

$$f'(x) = \frac{x^{\frac{2}{3}}}{3}\left[ax^p + bx^q + cx^r\right]$$

What is the value of $abc + pqr$?

A. 388
B. $\frac{520}{3}$
C. 288
D. 316
E. 300
F. -80

Question 171:

ABC is a triangle. You are told that the side AB has length 3cm, $\sin B = \frac{1}{\sqrt{2}}$ and $\sin C = \frac{\sqrt{3}}{2}$. How many different triangles can be formed from this information?

A. 0
B. 1
C. 2
D. 3
E. 4
F. 5
G. Infinitely many

Question 172:

Which of the following is the largest?

A. $\log_3 8$
B. $(1.4)^2$
C. $\frac{13}{6}$
D. $\sqrt{6}$
E. $\frac{\sqrt{15}}{\sqrt{5}+1}$

Question 173:

Let the line l have equation $y = \frac{x}{3} + 3$. Let l_2 be the line perpendicular to l at the point on l where $y = 8$. What is the area between the two lines, the x-axis and the y-axis?

    A. $\frac{169}{3}$

    B. $\frac{551}{6}$

    C. $\frac{559}{6}$

    D. $\frac{181}{2}$

    E.   70

Question 174:

Find the sum of the 2 distinct roots for x in the simultaneous equations:

$$\log_8 x + \log_8 y = \frac{1}{2}$$

$$(\log_8 x)(\log_8 y) = -5$$

    A. $2^{\frac{3}{2}}$

    B. $2^{\frac{15}{2}} + 2^{-6}$

    C. $2^{-7} - 2$

    D. $2^{-\frac{7}{2}}$

    E. $2^{\frac{3}{2}}$

    F. $2^{\frac{5}{2}} + 2^{-2}$

Question 175:

The volume of a cylinder is between 2 and 3 times the value of its overall surface area. If its height is 8, what values can r take? (Assuming r is non=zero)

    A. $1 \leq r \leq 3$

    B. $r \leq 8$

    C. $8 \leq r \leq 24$

    D. $r \geq 16$

    E. $\frac{3}{2} \leq r \leq \frac{7}{4}$

    F. $2 \leq r \leq 3$

Question 176:

On Mondays Professor X takes one of class A or class B. The probability he picks class A is $\frac{2}{7}$.

On Tuesdays, he takes class A if he took class B the day before, otherwise he picks in the same way he did on Monday.

Prof. X took class A on Tuesday; what is the probability he took class A on Monday?

    A. $\frac{2}{7}$

    B. $\frac{5}{7}$

    C. $\frac{10}{49}$

    D. $\frac{10}{39}$

    E. $\frac{4}{39}$

    F. $\frac{7}{39}$

    G. $\frac{31}{49}$

Question 177:

Every day, a man decides whether to walk his dog with probability $\frac{1}{3}$ that he does take it for a walk, independently of choices made on other days. After 4 days, what is the probability that he walked his dg at least once every 2 days?

    A. $\frac{1}{27}$

    B. $\frac{7}{27}$

    C. $\frac{8}{27}$

    D. $\frac{11}{27}$

    E. $\frac{1}{9}$

    F. $\frac{1}{3}$

Question 178:

A triangle ABC has angle $CAB = 45°$, and angle $ACB = 30°$. It also has side length $AB = 500$mm.

What is the area of this triangle?

There are infinitely many possible values

    A. $125^2(\sqrt{3} + \sqrt{2})$

    B. $250^2(\sqrt{3} + \sqrt{2})$

    C. $125^2(\sqrt{3} - 1)$

    D. $250^2(\sqrt{3} + 1)$

Question 179:

Consider the circle $x^2 + (y - 2)^2 = 4$. A straight line intersects the circle at the lower of the points where $x = \sqrt{3}$ such that the perimeter of the arc of the circle below the line is equal to $\frac{7\pi}{6}$. What is the equation of the line?

   A. $y = \left(\sqrt{6} - \sqrt{3} - \sqrt{2} + 2\right)x - \sqrt{18} + 2 - \sqrt{6} + 3\sqrt{3}$
   B. $y = \left(\sqrt{6} + \sqrt{3} + \sqrt{2} - 2\right)x - \sqrt{18} + 2 - \sqrt{6} - 3\sqrt{3}$
   C. $y = \left(\sqrt{6} - \sqrt{3} - \sqrt{2} - 2\right)x + \sqrt{18} + 2 - \sqrt{6} + 3\sqrt{3}$
   D. $y = \left(\sqrt{6} - \sqrt{3} + \sqrt{2} - 2\right)x - \sqrt{18} + 2 - \sqrt{6} + 3\sqrt{3}$
   E. $y = \left(\sqrt{6} - \sqrt{3} + \sqrt{2} - 2\right)x - \sqrt{18} - 2 - \sqrt{6} + 3\sqrt{3}$

Question 180:

Given that $\frac{dy}{dt} = 2t^{-3} + \frac{3 - t^2}{t^{-2}}, t \neq 0$

And that $y = 2$ when $t = 1$, find y in terms of t.

   A. $y = \frac{17}{6} + t^3 - \frac{t^5}{5} + \frac{t^{-4}}{2}$
   B. $y = \frac{17}{10} + t^3 - \frac{t^5}{5} - \frac{t^{-4}}{2}$
   C. $y = \frac{3}{10} - t^3 - \frac{t^5}{5} - \frac{t^{-4}}{2}$
   D. $y = \frac{17}{6} + t^3 - \frac{t^5}{5} - \frac{t^{-4}}{2}$
   E. $y = \frac{17}{6} + 2t^3 + \frac{t^5}{5} - \frac{t^{-4}}{2}$

Question 181:

The function $f(x) = \frac{\log_7 x}{3}$ is stretched by a factor of 8 parallel to the x-axis.

This stretch is equivalent to a translation in the y-direction by a. What is the value of a?

   A. $\frac{\log_7 4}{3}$
   B. 2
   C. $-\frac{1}{2}$
   D. $\log_7 2$
   E. 7
   F. 49
   G. -343

Question 182:

What is the shortest distance between these two circles?

$$x^2 + y^2 - 14x - 4y + 44 = 0$$

$$x^2 + y^2 + 6x + 8y = 0$$

A. 0
B. $2\sqrt{11} - 8$
C. 44
D. $2\sqrt{26} - 8$
E. $2\sqrt{34} - 8$
F. 64
G. $6\sqrt{7} + 5$

Question 183:

There is a box that is 3 m by 4 m by 5 m. What is the maximum length of stick that can fit in this box?

A. 6 m
B. $5\sqrt{2}$ m
C. $\sqrt{77}$ m
D. $2\sqrt{3}$ m
E. $\sqrt{39}$ m

Section 1B

Advanced Maths

Section 1B tests principles of advanced mathematics. You have to answer 20 questions in 30 minutes. The questions can be quite difficult and it's easy to get bogged down. However, it's well worth spending time preparing for this section as its possible to rapidly improve with targeted preparation.

Gaps in Knowledge

You are highly advised to go through the ECAA Specification and ensure that you have covered all examinable topics. An electronic copy of this can be obtained from uniadmissions.co.uk/ecaa. The questions in this book will help highlight any particular areas of weakness or gaps in your knowledge that you may have. Upon discovering these, make sure you take some time to revise these topics before carrying on – there is little to be gained by attempting these questions with huge gaps in your knowledge. A summary of the major topics is given below:

Algebra:

- Laws of Indices
- Manipulation of Surds
- Quadratic Functions: Graphs, use of discriminant, completing the square
- Solving Simultaneous Equations via Substitution
- Solving Linear and Quadratic Inequalities
- Manipulation of polynomials e.g. expanding brackets, factorising
- Use of Factor Theorem + Remainder Theorem

Graphing Functions:

- Sketching of common functions including lines, quadratics, cubics, trigonometric functions, logarithmic functions and exponential functions
- Manipulation of functions using simple transformations

Exponentials & Logs:

- Graph of $y = a^x$ series
- Law of Logarithms:
  - $a^b = c \leftrightarrow b = log_a c$
  - $log_a x + log_a y = log_a(xy)$
  - $log_a x - log_a y = log_a(\frac{x}{y})$
  - $k\ log_a x = log_a(x^k)$
  - $log_a \frac{1}{x} = -log_a x$
  - $log_a a = 1$

Trigonometry:

- Sine and Cosine rules
- Solution of trigonometric identities
- Values of sin, cost, tan for 0, 30, 45, 60 and 90 degrees
- Sine, Cosine, Tangent graphs, symmetries, periodicities
- $Area\ of\ Triangle\ = \frac{1}{2} ab \sin C$
- $\sin^2 \theta + \cos^2 q = 1$
- $tan\theta = \frac{sin\theta}{\cos \theta}$

Differentiation:

- First order and second order derivatives
- Familiarity with notation: $\frac{dy}{dx}, \frac{d^2y}{dx^2}, f'(x), f''(x)$
- Differentiation of functions like $y = x^n$

Integration:

- Definite and indefinite integrals for $y = x^n$
- Solving Differential Equations in the form: $\frac{dy}{dx} = f(x)$
- Understanding of the Fundamental Theorem of Calculus and its application:
    - $\int_a^b f(x)dx = F(b) - F(a), where\ F'(x) = f(x)$
    - $\frac{d}{dx}\int_a^x f(t)dt = f(x)$

Geometry:

- Circle Properties:
    - The angle subtended by an arc at the centre of a circle is double the size of the angle subtended by the arc on the circumference
    - The opposite angles in a cyclic quadrilateral summate to 180 degrees
    - The angle between the tangent and chord at the point of contact is equal to the angle in the alternate segment
    - The tangent at any point on a circle is perpendicular to the radius at that point
    - Triangles formed using the full diameter are right-angled triangles
    - Angles in the same segment are equal
    - The Perpendicular from the centre to a chord bisects the chord
- Equations for a circle:
    - $(x - a)^2 + (y - b)^2 = r^2$
    - $x^2 + y^2 + cx + dy + e = 0$
- Equations for a straight line:
    - $y - y_1 = m(x - x_1)$
    - $Ax + by + c = 0$

Series:

- Arithmetic series and Geometric Series
- Summing to a finite and infinite geometric series
- Binomial Expansions
- Factorials

Formulas you MUST know:

2D Shapes			3D Shapes		
Area				Surface Area	Volume
Circle	πr2	Cuboid	Sum of all 6 faces	Length x width x height
Parallelogram	Base x Vertical height	Cylinder	2 πr2 + 2πrl	πr2 x l
Trapezium	0.5 x h x (a+b)	Cone	πr2 + πrl	πr2 x (h/3)
Triangle	0.5 x base x height	Sphere	4 πr2	(4/3) πr3

Even good students who are studying maths at A level can struggle with certain ECAA maths topics because they're usually glossed over at school. These include:

Quadratic Formula

The solutions for a quadratic equation in the form $ax^2 + bx + c = 0$ are given by: $x = \frac{-b \pm \sqrt{b^2 - 4ac}}{2a}$

Remember that you can also use the discriminant to quickly see if a quadratic equation has any solutions:

$$If\ b^2 - 4ac < 0: No\ solutions$$

$$If\ b^2 - 4ac = 0: One\ solution$$

$$If\ b^2 - 4ac > 2: Two\ solutions$$

Completing the Square

If a quadratic equation cannot be factorised easily and is in the format $ax^2 + bx + c = 0$ then you can rearrange it into the form $a\left(x + \frac{b}{2a}\right)^2 + \left[c - \frac{b^2}{4a}\right] = 0$

This looks more complicated than it is – remember that in the ECAA, you're extremely unlikely to get quadratic equations where $a > 1$ and the equation doesn't have any easy factors. This gives you an easier equation: $\left(x + \frac{b}{2}\right)^2 + \left[c - \frac{b^2}{4}\right] = 0$ and is best understood with an example.

Consider: $x^2 + 6x + 10 = 0$

This equation cannot be factorised easily but note that: $x^2 + 6x - 10 = (x + 3)^2 - 19 = 0$

Therefore, $x = -3 \pm \sqrt{19}$. Completing the square is an important skill – make sure you're comfortable with it.

Difference between 2 Squares

If you are asked to simplify expressions and find that there are no common factors but it involves square numbers – you might be able to factorise by using the 'difference between two squares'.

For example, $x^2 - 25$ can also be expressed as $(x + 5)(x - 5)$.

Advanced Maths Questions

Question 184:

What is the coefficient of x^3 in the expansion of $(2 - x)^2(2 + x)^4(x - 2)^2$?

   A. 16
   B. 8
   C. 0
   D. -8
   E. -16

Question 185:

Evaluate the following integral: $\int_3^4 \frac{1}{x^2+x-6}\,dx$

   A. $0.2\ln\left(\frac{12}{7}\right)$
   B. $0.2\ln\left(\frac{12}{14}\right)$
   C. $-0.2\ln\left(\frac{12}{14}\right)$
   D. $0.2\ln\left(\frac{6}{7}\right)$
   E. $-0.2\ln\left(\frac{12}{9}\right)$

Question 186:

What is the second derivative of $f(x) = e^{-2x} + x^2$?

   A. $4e^{-2x} + 2$
   B. $4e^{-2x} - 2$
   C. $2e^{-2x} + 2$
   D. $e^{-2x} + 2$
   E. $2e^{-2x} - 2$

Question 187:

Find the equation of the tangent to the curve $y = 3x^2$ at point (1,3).

   A. $y = 6x + 3$
   B. $y = 3x - 3$
   C. $y = 6x - 6$
   D. $y = 6x - 3$
   E. $y = -6x + 3$

Question 188:

Differentiate $y = \frac{\sin(2x+5)}{x^2+6x}$ with respect to x.

A. $\frac{2(\cos(2x+5))(x^2+6x)-\sin(2x+5)(2x+6)}{(x^2-6x)^2}$

B. $\frac{2(\cos(2x+5))(x^2+6x)+\sin(2x+5)(2x+6)}{(x^2+6x)^2}$

C. $\frac{2(\cos(2x+5))(x^2+6x)-\sin(2x+5)(2x+6)}{(x^2+6x)^2}$

D. $\frac{2(\sin(2x+5))(x^2+6x)-\sin(2x+5)(2x+6)}{(x^2+6x)^2}$

E. $\frac{2(\cos(2x+5))(x^2+6x)-\cos(2x+5)(2x+6)}{(x^2+6x)^2}$

Question 189:

Evaluate the following sum:

$$1 + \tfrac{1}{2} + \tfrac{1}{4} + \ldots$$

A. 1.75
B. 2
C. 2.25
D. 2.5
E. 3

Question 190:

Find the roots of $x^3 - 7x + 6$ by factorising it.

A. 3, 2, and -1
B. 3, 2, and 1
C. -3, 2, and 1
D. 3, -2, and 1
E. -3, -2, and -1

Question 191:

Find the derivative of $f(x) = 2\cos x + x^2$.

A. $2\sin x + 2x$
B. $-2\sin x + 2x$
C. $-2\sin x - 2x$
D. $-2\cos x + 2x$
E. $2\cos x + 2x$

Question 192:

If a 1000 km tall skyscraper was built, what would be the ratio of your weight at the top of it to your weight on the ground? The radius of earth is 6371 km.

     A. $\dfrac{6371^2}{7371^2}$

     B. $\dfrac{6370^2}{7370^2}$

     C. $\dfrac{7370^2}{6370^2}$

     D. $\dfrac{6370}{7370}$

     E. $\dfrac{6371}{7371}$

Question 193:

A ball of mass m is attached to two springs of spring constant k connected in parallel that can be extended by a length L. What is the maximum speed of oscillations?

     A. $\sqrt{\dfrac{k}{m}}\,L$

     B. $\sqrt{\dfrac{k}{2m}}\,L$

     C. $\sqrt{\dfrac{2k}{m}}\,L$

     D. $\sqrt{\dfrac{k}{m^2}}\,L$

     E. $\sqrt{\dfrac{k^2}{2m}}\,L$

Question 194:

At constant pressure, an ideal monoatomic gas was compressed to half its original volume. How did its temperature change?

     A. T_1

     B. $\dfrac{1}{2}T_1$

     C. $\dfrac{1}{4}T_1$

     D. $2T_1$

     E. $\dfrac{1}{8}T_1$

Question 195:

A ray of light travelling in the air is incident at an angle of $60°$ to a layer of water. If then travels through the layer of water ($n = 1.34$) until it reaches a layer of oil ($n = 1.55$). Find the angle of refraction at the water-oil boundary.

     A. 60°

     B. 55°

C. 45°
D. 42°
E. 34°

Question 196:

Find the tangent to $y = \sqrt{8x - 4x^2}$ at $x = 2$.

A. $x = 2$
B. $y = 2$
C. $y = 2x$
D. $y = 2x+2$
E. $y = -2$

Question 197:

Let $f(x)$ be a function defined over all real x. You are given that $\int_2^5 2f(2x)dx = 1$, and that $f(x)$ is antisymmettric in the line $\frac{3}{2}$, ie $f\left(\frac{3}{2} - x\right) = -f(x)$. Calculate $\int_2^3 f(x) + 1 \, dx$.

Not enough information

A. 2
B. 4
C. 0
D. $\sqrt{2}$

Question 198:

If p is a prime number, which of the following **must** be true?

I.   p is odd
II.   p is not divisible by 5
III. p is not divisible by 6

A. I only
B. II only
C. III only
D. I and III only
E. II and III only

Question 199:

Let I, II, III, IV be some statements. Suppose that $I \to II \to III$ and $IV \to Not\ III$ and $Not\ I \to II$, where $a \to b$ means if a is true, then b is true. *not a* is just the opposite to a, so if a is true, *Not a* is false and vice versa.

Suppose II is a true statement. What can we say about the rest of the statements?

	I	III	IV
A	true	true	true
B	could be either	true	could be either
C	could be either	true	false
D	false	true	false
E	true	false	false

Question 200:

Let $f(x) = ax^7 + bx^6 + cx^5 + dx^4 + ex^3 + fx^2 + gx + h$, with a, b, c, d, e, f, g, h real constants, and $a > 0$. Which of the following is possible?

    A. Graph has 1 maxima and 0 minima
    B. Graph has 2 maxima and 3 minima
    C. Graph has 7 maxima and 7 minima
    D. Graph has 1 maxima and 1 minima
    E. Graph has 0 maxima and 1 minima

Question 201:

What is the coefficient of x^2 in the expansion of $(1 + x)^2 \left(\frac{2}{x^2} - 3x^2\right)^4$

    A. 81
    B. 100
    C. 121
    D. 144
    E. 225

Question 202:

Let I and II be two statements. You are asked to show that I if and only if II. Which of the following does **not** prove the statement

    A. II if I, and I if II
    B. *not I* if II, and *not II* if I
    C. *not II* if *not I*, and *not I* if *not II*
    D. *not I* if *not II*, and I if II

Question 203:

Which of the following are necessary and sufficient conditions for the equations $y = x - 4$ and $x^2 - 2y^2 = a$ to have solutions

  A. $a < 32$
  B. $a \leq 32$
  C. $a > 32$
  D. $a \geq 32$
  E. $a < 16$
  F. $a \leq 16$
  G. $a > 16$
  H. $a \geq 16$

Question 204:

Consider the statement: "If n is an integer and n^2 is divisible by 4, then n is divisible by 4"

How many counterexamples are there to this in the range $50 \leq n \leq 100$.

  A. 24
  B. 25
  C. 11
  D. 12
  E. 13

Question 205:

It is given that a certain equation $f(x) = 0$ has n roots. Which of the following must be true?

  I. $f(x + 1)$ has n roots F
  II. $2f(2x + 2)$ has n roots F
  III. $f(x) + 1$ has n $roots$ T
  IV. $2^{f(x)} - 1 = 0$ has n roots
  A. II and IV
  B. I and II
  C. All true
  D. I, II and IV
  E. I and III

Question 206:

Calculate the derivative of $(1 + 4x)^3 (2x)^{-\frac{1}{2}}$

  A. $\dfrac{(4x+1)^2 (15x+1)}{2^{\frac{3}{2}} x^{\frac{3}{2}}}$

  B. $\dfrac{(4x+1)^2 (15x-1)}{2^{\frac{3}{2}} x^{\frac{3}{2}}}$

  C. $\dfrac{(4x+1)^2 (20x-1)}{2^{\frac{3}{2}} x^{\frac{3}{2}}}$

D. $\dfrac{(4x+1)^2(20x+1)}{2^{\frac{1}{2}}x^{\frac{3}{2}}}$

E. $\dfrac{(4x+1)^2(20x+1)}{2^{\frac{3}{2}}x^{\frac{1}{2}}}$

Question 207:

Let f be a function satisfying the following condition: for all x_1, x_2 and for $0 \le t \le 1$,

$$f(tx_1 + (1-t)x_2 \le tf(x_1) + (1-t)f(x_2)$$

Which of the following is a necessary condition for this to hold?

A. f(x) ≥ 0 for all real x
B. f (x) ≥ 0 for all real x
C. f'(x) ≥ 0 for all real x
D. f'(x) ≤ 0 for all real x
E. f''(x) ≤ 0 for all real x
F. f''(x) ≥ 0 for all real x

Question 208:

A geometric series has first term $a = \sqrt{32}$ and 6th term $1/a^2$. Find the sum to infinity.

A. $\dfrac{16}{\sqrt{2}+2}$

B. $\dfrac{16}{2\sqrt{2}+1}$

C. $\dfrac{16+32\sqrt{2}}{7}$

D. $\dfrac{16-32\sqrt{2}}{7}$

E. $\dfrac{16+16\sqrt{2}}{7}$

Question 209:

A large circular room has 2020 light bulbs attached to the edge. Each light bulb has a switch below it, that controls the state of the two adjacent light bulbs to it. Given that all the light bulbs start off, how many can be turned on at once?

A. 1010
B. 1515
C. 2020
D. 2019
E. 2018

Question 210:

Evaluate the sum

$$\left(1 + \frac{1}{3} + \frac{1}{9} + \frac{1}{27} + \cdots\right) + \left(\frac{1}{3} + \frac{1}{9} + \frac{1}{27} + \cdots\right) + \left(\frac{1}{9} + \frac{1}{27} + \cdots\right) + \cdots$$

   A. $\frac{3}{2}$

   B. $\frac{9}{4}$

   C. $\frac{5}{9}$

   D. $\frac{12}{9}$

   E. The series diverges

Question 211:

A student attempts to solve the following equation:

$$\frac{x^2 - 5x + 6}{x^2 + x + 1} = \frac{x^2 - 5x + 6}{2x^2 - 3x - 2}$$

By using the following steps:

$$\frac{1}{x^2 + x + 1} = \frac{1}{2x^2 - 3x - 2}$$

$$x^2 + x + 1 = 2x^2 - 3x - 2$$

$$x^2 + 2x - 3 = 0$$

$$x = -3, 1$$

Which of the following best describes the solution?

   A. The method is completely correct
   B. The method is incorrect and from a to b we have introduced extra solutions
   C. The method is incorrect and we are missing 1 solution
   D. The solutions given are incorrect
   E. The method is incorrect and we are missing 2 solutions

Question 212:

Find a necessary and sufficient condition on a, such that $\sqrt{a - \sqrt{a - \sqrt{a - \cdots}}} = \dfrac{1}{a - \dfrac{1}{a - \dfrac{1}{a - \cdots}}}$

   A. True for all real a
   B. $a = 0$
   C. $a = 1$
   D. $a = 2$
   E. $a = \sqrt{2}$

Question 213:

Let n be a positive integer. Which of the following statements are always true?

    I. $n^3 - n$ is divisible by 6
    II. $n^3 - n$ is divisible by 4
   III. $n^3 - n$ is never prime

    A. All of them
    B. Only I
    C. Only II
    D. I and II
    E. I and III

Question 214:

Let $A = \int_0^1 \sin x \, dx$, $B = \int_0^1 \sin^2 x \, dx$, $C = \int_0^1 \cos x \, dx$, $D = \int_0^1 \cos^2 x \, dx$. Order the integrals

    A. $D < A < C < B$
    B. $C < B < A < D$
    C. $D < B < C < A$
    D. $D < A < B < C$
    E. $D < B < A < C$

Question 215:

How many solutions in $0 \leq x \leq 2\pi$ are there to the following equation?

$$\tan^2 3x = \frac{1}{\cos 3x}$$

    A. 0
    B. 1
    C. 2
    D. 3
    E. 4
    F. 6
    G. 9
    H. 12

Question 216:

A student tried to solve the following problem:

$$\frac{2^{18x}}{2^{3x^2}4^6} > 1$$

Here is his solution:

    I. $\frac{2^{18x}}{2^{3x^2}4^6} = 2^{18x-3x^2}4^{-6} > 1$

   II. $8^{6x-3x^2}4^{-6} > 1$

III. $8^{6x-x^2-3} > 1$

IV. $6x - x^2 - 3 > 0$

V.   Critical values are $x = \frac{6 \pm \sqrt{36-12}}{2} = 3 \pm \sqrt{6}$

VI.   So $3 - \sqrt{6} < x < 3 + \sqrt{6}$

Where is the first error?

- A. The proof is correct
- B. Line (I)
- C. Line (II)
- D. Line (III)
- E. Line (IV)
- F. Line (V)
- G. Line (VI)

Question 217:

Consider the following proof by contradiction that $\sqrt{12}$ is irrational.

I.   Suppose $\sqrt{12}$ is irrational. The we can express it in the form $\sqrt{12} = \frac{a}{b}$ for some a and b with no common divisors.

II. $12 = \frac{a^2}{b^2}$

III. $12b^2 = a^2$

IV.   12 divides a^2, which means that 12 must also divide a i.e. $a = 12c$ for some integer c.

V.   This means $144c^2 = 12b^2$ i.e. $b^2 = 12c^2$

VI.   Using the logic of line (IV), $b = 12d$ for some integer d.

VII.   But then a and d both have 12 as a divisor, which is a contradiction.

Where is the first error?

The proof is correct.

- A. Line (I)
- B. Line (II)
- C. Line (IV)
- D. Line (V)
- E. Line (VI)
- F. Line (VII)

Question 218:

A polynomial $f(x)$ has 3 roots at $x = p, q, r$ where $p < q < r$. Which of the following statements are sometimes true, never true, or always true, based on the above information?

I. $f(x + r)$ has fewer positive roots than $f(x)$

II. $f(x) - f(r)$ has no roots

III. $f(x) + 1$ has no roots.

	I	II	III
A	Always	Always	Sometimes
B	Always	Never	Sometimes
C	Always	Sometimes	Never
D	Sometimes	Never	Sometimes
E	Sometimes	Sometimes	Sometimes
F	Never	Always	Never

Question 219

Consider the graph of the curve $y = a(x + b)^2 + c$ where all of $a, b, c > 0$. Now suppose that a decreases and c increases. Which of the following graphs can it not be now?

A. I only
B. II only
C. III only
D. IV only
E. I & II only
F. I & III only
G. II & IV only
H. III & IV only

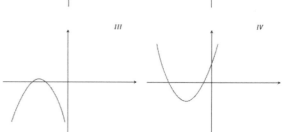

Question 220:

Find the coefficient of x^3 in the expansion of $(x^2 - 2)^3(1 + (3x)^{-1})^4$.

A. $\dfrac{220}{27}$

B. $\dfrac{4}{27}$

C. $-\dfrac{24}{3}$

D. $-\dfrac{212}{27}$

E. $\dfrac{100}{27}$

Question 221:

Which of the following is a counterexample to the statement below?

If a function has 3 distinct real roots, it is cubic.

A. $\sin x$ in the range $0 < x < 2pi$
B. $(x - 1)(x - 2)(x - 3)(x - 4)$
C. $\cos x$ in the range $0 < x < 2pi$
D. $(x - 1)^2(x - 2)(x - 3)$
E. $(x + 1)(x^2 - x + 5)$
F. $(x - 3)(x + 1)(x - 4)$

Question 222:

Consider this student's attempt at finding the solutions to $\sqrt{x + 3} = 3x - 1$:

  I. $x + 3 = (3x - 1)^2$
  II. $x + 3 = 9x^2 - 6x + 1$
  III. $0 = 9x^2 - 7x - 2$
  IV. $0 = (x - 1)(9x + 2)$
  V.   So $x = 1$ and $- 2/9$

Is this correct?

Both answers are correct.

  A. Only one is right and it's due to an error in line (I).
  B. Only one is right and it's due to an error in lines (II) and (III).
  C. Only one is right and it's due to an error in line (IV).
  D. Neither is right and it's due to an error in line (I).
  E. Neither is right and it's due to an error in lines (II) and (III).
  F. Neither is right and it's due to an error in line (IV).

Question 223:

Consider the graphs of the two functions $y = mx + 10$ and $y = \log_2 x$. Which of the following correctly identifies the

sufficiency and necessity of

  I. $m < 0$
  II. $m > 10$

in relation to the statement that there are no intersection points of the two graphs?

  A. Both necessary and sufficient.
  B. Both necessary.
  C. Both sufficient.
  D. 1 is sufficient, the other is necessary.
  E. Only 1 is necessary.
  F. Only 1 is sufficient.
  G. Neither is necessary or sufficient.

Question 224:

Let f be a function such that $f(x) \leq 0$ for all $x \geq 0$. Which one of the following is necessary for $\int_{-1}^{1} f(x)dx > 0$?

  A. $f(x) = -f(-x)$ for all x
  B. $f(0) = 0$
  C. $f(x) \geq 0$ for all $x < 0$
  D. $\int_{-a}^{0} f(x)dx > 0$ for some a

E. $f(x) = f(-x)$ for all x

F. $f(-1) > 0$

Question 225:

Let $f(x) = ax^2$ and let $\int_{-b}^{b} f(x)dx = R$. Find the area between the curve $f(x - b) - f(b)$ and the x-axis.

A. $f(b) - R$

B. $f(b) - 2R$

C. $3R + f(b) + b$

D. $f(b) - 2bR$

E. R

F. $2bf(b) - R$

Question 226:

A function $f(x)$ has exactly 1 root in the range $0 < x < 2\pi$. Which of the following can not be the function in question?

A. $f(x) = \tan\frac{5x}{7}$

B. $f(x) = \log_{2.9} x$

C. $f(x) = \cos x + 1$

D. $f(x) = \sin x - 1$

E. $f(x) = 3^x$

Question 227:

Consider the following proof by induction that $3 \times 7^n + 6$ is divisible by 9 for all non-negative n:

I. Check the base case, $n = 1$; $3 \times 7 + 6 = 27$, which is indeed divisible by 9.

II. First, we suppose $3 \times 7^n + 6$ is divisible by 9 for $n \le k$. i.e. $3 \times 7^k + 6 = 9M$ for some integer M.

III. Then $3 \times 7^{k+1} + 6 = 7 \times (3 \times 7^k) + 6$

IV. This means $7 \times (3 \times 7^k) + 6 = 7(9M - 6) + 6$

V. Which means $3 \times 7^{k+1} + 6 = 9(7M - 4)$

VI. So $3 \times 7^{k+1} + 6$ is also divisible by 9, which means $3 \times 7^n + 6$ is divisible by 9 for all non-negative n

Where is the first error?

A. The proof is correct.

B. Line (I)

C. Line (II)

D. Line (III)

E. Line (IV)

F. Line (V)

G. Line (VI)

Question 228:

I have a 5 character code for my safe, which is formed by the letters a, b, c, d, e in some order (each occurs only once) and for every wrong attempt, my safe will tell me how many of the characters were in the correct position.

Which of the following can never occur?

I. I enter $abcde, bcdea, cdeab$ and the safe tells me I got 2 correct on all 3.
II. I enter $cdaeb, acebd, abecd$ and the safe tells me I got 1, then 2, then 3 correct respectively.
III. I enter $abcde, bacde$ and the safe tells me I got 3 correct on both.

A. None
B. I only
C. II only
D. III only
E. I & II only
F. I & III only
G. II & III only
H. All three

Question 229:

Suppose there is a function $f(x)$, and $\int_0^7 |x - p| f(x)dx = A$, for some $0 \le p \le 7$. Which of the following is a valid formula for A? $\left[F_1 = \int (x - p)f(x)dx\right]$?

A. $F_1(7) - F_1(0)$
B. $F_1(7) - pF_1(0)$
C. $F_1(0) - pF_1(7)$
D. $2F_1(0) - F_1(7) + F_1(p)$
E. $F_1(7) + F_1(0) - 2F_1(p)$
F. $F_1(p) + F_1(7) - 2F_1(0)$

Question 230:

Suppose you have a sphere, S. The cylinder C is such that S fits entirely inside C, and the volume of C is as small as possible. The surface area of C is $B cm^2$.

Which of the following is an expression for the volume of S in terms of B? (The volume of a sphere of radius r is $\frac{4\pi r^3}{3}$)

A. $\frac{2B}{9}$
B. $\frac{2B}{9\pi}$
C. $\frac{B^{\frac{3}{2}}\sqrt{2}}{9\sqrt{3\pi}}$
D. $\frac{2B^{\frac{3}{2}}}{27\pi}$
E. B^3
F. $\frac{B^3}{2}$

Question 231:

I have a bag with many tiles in, each of which has one integer written on it. I pick a tile out of the bag at random. $P(\text{the number is odd}) = \frac{1}{3}$ and $P(\text{the number is prime}) = \frac{1}{5}$.

Consider the following statements:

   I. $P(\text{number is even}) - P(\text{the number is 2}) = \frac{4}{5}$

  II. $P(\text{the number is not prime and is even}) = \frac{8}{15}$

 III. $P(\text{the number is not prime and is odd}) = \frac{2}{15} + P(\text{the number is 2})$

Which of these statements are definitely true?

  A. None
  B. I only
  C. II only
  D. III only
  E. I & II only
  F. I & III only
  G. II & III only
  H. All three

Question 232:

Suppose that the equation $\sqrt{xp} = x + \sqrt{p}$ has exactly 1 solution for x. How many valid values of p are there?

Infinitely many (i.e. an interval)

  A. 4
  B. 3
  C. 2
  D. 1
  E. 0
  F. None

Question 233:

A woman tosses a fair coin 10 times and records the outcome, with an H for a head, and T for a tail. The sequence she creates is $H\ T\ T\ T\ T\ T\ T\ H\ T\ H\ H$. The probability that this occurred was p.

Which of the following are true if she was to repeat what she did?

  I. $P(\text{more than 4 heads appearing}) > \frac{1}{2}$

 II. $P(\text{7 tails appearing}) < p$

III. $P(\text{same sequence}) = p$

  A. None
  B. I only
  C. II only

D. III only
E. I & II only
F. I & III only
G. II & III only
H. All three

Question 234:

Find the sum of the values of a such that the quartic equation

$$x^4 - x^3 - \frac{x^2}{2} = a$$

Has an odd number of solutions.

A. $\frac{3}{4}$

B. $-\frac{1}{2}$

C. There are no values of a.

D. $-\frac{139}{256}$

E. $\frac{117}{256}$

F. $-\frac{117}{256}$

Question 235:

Differentiate $y = 5x^2 \sin 2x$ with respect to x.

A. $10x(x \cos2x - \sin 2x)$
B. $10x(x \cos2x + \sin 2x)$
C. $10x(x^2 \cos2x + \sin 2x)$
D. $5x(x \cos2x + \sin 2x)$
E. $10x(x \sin2x + \cos 2x)$

Question 236:

If $x = 1$ is a root of equation $2x^3 + x^2 - 5x = -2$, find the other two roots.

A. $x = 1$ and $x = -2$
B. $x = \frac{1}{2}$ and $x = 2$
C. $x = \frac{1}{2}$ and $x = 1$
D. $x = \frac{1}{2}$ and $x = -2$
E. $x = -\frac{1}{2}$ and $x = -2$

Question 237:

Evaluate the following sum: $\sum_{n=0}^{4} 3^{-n}$

A. $\frac{112}{81}$

B. $\frac{121}{81}$

C. $\dfrac{121}{80}$

D. $\dfrac{120}{81}$

E. $\dfrac{121}{41}$

Question 238:

If $\dfrac{\log_2 8^x}{\log_3 9^y} = 12$ and $3x + 5y = 10$, what is $\log_x y$?

A. $\dfrac{80}{29}$

B. $\dfrac{80}{22}$

C. $\dfrac{60}{29}$

D. $\dfrac{40}{29}$

E. $\dfrac{80}{28}$

Question 239:

Evaluate the following integral: $\int_0^5 \dfrac{6x}{3x^2+5} dx$

A. $\ln(10)$

B. $\ln(12)$

C. $\ln(16)$

D. $-\ln(16)$

E. $-\ln(20)$

Question 240:

What is the function of the following graph?

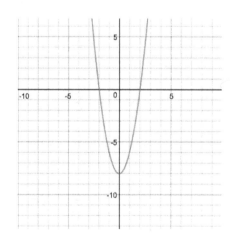

A. $y = x^2 - 8$

B. $y = 2x^2 + 8$

C. $y = 2x^2 - 8$

D. $y = 2x^2 - 6$

E. $y = x^2 + 8$

Question 241:

What is the coefficient of x^6 in the expansion of $(1 - 2x)^3(2 + x)^4$?

    A. $54x^6$
    B. $-54x^6$
    C. $-52x^6$
    D. $-50x^6$
    E. $50x^6$

Question 242:

What is x in the equation $\log_3 x^2 + \log_4 \frac{1}{64} = 3$?

    A. 18
    B. 21
    C. 27
    D. 30
    E. 33

Question 244:

What is the equation of a line that connects the points (-3,5) and (2,-6)?

    A. $5y + 11x = 8$
    B. $-5y + 11x = -8$
    C. $5y - 11x = -8$
    D. $5y + 11x = -8$
    E. $5y - 11x = 8$

Question 245:

Evaluate the sum of the following sequence 1+3+5+…..+99.

    A. 1500
    B. 2000
    C. 2250
    D. 2500
    E. 2750

Question 246:

How many numbers greater than 3000 may be formed by using some or all of the digits 1,2,3,4, and 5 without repetition?

    A. 144
    B. 160
    C. 176
    D. 188
    E. 192

Question 247:

Evaluate: $(6 \sin x)(3 \sin x) - (9 \cos x)(-2 \cos x)$

A. 0
B. 0.5
C. 1
D. -1
E. 18
F. -18

Question 248:

In the figure to the right, all triangles are equilateral. What is the shaded area of the figure in terms of r?

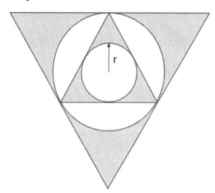

A. $5r^2(2\sqrt{6} - 3\pi)$
B. $5r^2(5\sqrt{2} - 6\pi)$
C. $5r^2(3\sqrt{3} - \pi)$
D. $5r^2(4\sqrt{3} - 2\pi)$
E. $5r(2\sqrt{6 - 3\pi})$
F. $5r^2(5\sqrt{2} + 6\pi)$

Question 249:

Suppose I use a binomial expansion to determine the value of $(3.12)^5$. What is the minimum number of terms that I must obtain in the expansion of $(3.12)^5$ in order to receive a result accurate to 1 decimal place?

A. 4
B. 5
C. 6
D. 7
E. 9
F. 8

Question 250:

For all θ, $(\sin(\theta) + \sin(-\theta))(\cos(\theta) + \cos(-\theta)) =$

A. $2 \sin \theta$
B. 0

C. 1

D. $4 \sin \theta \cos \theta$

E. -1

F. $2 sin\theta cos\theta$

Question 251:

What is the range of values for which the inequality $|2x - 5| > 3|2x + 1|$ is valid?

A. $-2 < x < 4$

B. $x > -2, x > \frac{1}{4}$

C. $-2 < x < \frac{1}{4}$

D. $x > -2, x > 4$

E. $-2 < x < 4$

F. $x > -2$

Question 252:

Which of the following is the equation of the circle whose diameter is the line segment connecting points $(1, -4)$ and $(3,6)$ and is reflected about the line $y = x$?

A. $(x + 4)^2 + (y - 1)^2 = 104$

B. $(x - 1)^2 + (y + 4)^2 = 104$ ✕

C. $(x - 1)^2 + (y - 2)^2 = 26$

D. $(x - 2)^2 + (y - 1)^2 = 2$

E. $(x+1)^2 + (y + 2)^2 = 26$

F. $(x + 2)^2 + (y + 1)^2 = 2$

Question 253:

A new computer does a calculation in b hours, and an old computer does c calculations in d minutes.

If the two computers work together, how many calculations can they perform in m minutes?

A. $60m \left(\frac{a}{b} + \frac{c}{d} \right)$

B. $m \left(\frac{60a}{b} + \frac{c}{d} \right)$

C. $m \left(\frac{a}{b} + \frac{c}{d} \right)$

D. $m \left(\frac{a}{60b} + \frac{c}{d} \right)$

E. $2m \left(\frac{30a}{b} + \frac{c}{d} \right)$

F. $m \left(\frac{a}{60b} + \frac{d}{c} \right)$

Question 254:

If -1 is a zero of the function $f(x) = 2x^3 + 3x^2 - 20x - 21$, then what are the other zeroes?

A. 1 and 3

B. -3 and 3

C. $-\frac{7}{2}$ and 1 and 3

D. $-\frac{7}{2}$ and 3

E. -1 and 3

F. 1 and 7

Question 255:

The three roots of third order polynomial are -1, 0 and 1. Find one of the possible polynomials.

A. $x^3 - x + 1$

B. $x^3 - 2x - 3$

C. $x^3 + x$

D. $x^3 - x$

E. $x^3 - x - 6$

Question 256:

Given the two equations $y_1 = (1 - x)^6$ and $y_2 = (1 + 2x)^6$, find the ratio of the coefficients of the 2$^\text{nd}$ term in the expansion of y_1 and the 3$^\text{rd}$ term in the expansion of y_2 (The y_1 coefficient should be the numerator, and the y_2 coefficient should be the denominator).

A. $-\frac{1}{10}$

B. $\frac{1}{9}$

C. $\frac{1}{15}$

D. $-\frac{1}{7}$

Question 257:

What is the sum of the integers from 1 to 300?

A. 9,000

B. 44,850

C. 45,150

D. 45,450

E. 54,450

F. 90,000

Question 258:

If $\sin 2\theta = \frac{2}{5}$, then what is $\frac{1}{\sin \theta \cos \theta}$?

A. $\frac{1}{5}$

B. $\frac{5}{4}$

C. $\frac{5}{2}$

D. 5

E. $\frac{3}{2}$

F. 1

Question 259:

If $\lfloor n \rfloor$ represents the greatest integer less than or equal to n, then which of the following is the solution to $-11 + 4\lfloor n \rfloor = 5$?

A. $n = 4$

B. $4 < n < 5$

C. $-2 \leq n \leq -1$

D. $4 \leq n < 5$

E. $4 < n \leq 5$

F. $4 < n \leq 5$

Question 260:

Rearrange the following to make m the subject.

A. $T = 4\pi\sqrt{\dfrac{(M+3m)l}{3(M+2m)g}}$

B. $m = \dfrac{16\pi^2 lM - 3gMT^2}{48\pi^2 l - 6gT^2}$

C. $m = \dfrac{16\pi^2 lM - 3gMT^2}{6gT^2 - 48\pi^2 l}$

D. $m = \dfrac{3gMT^2 - 16\pi^2 lM}{6gT^2 - 48\pi^2 l}$

E. $m = \dfrac{4\pi^2 lM - 3gMT^2}{6gT^2 - 16\pi^2 l}$

F. $m = \left(\dfrac{16\pi^2 lM - 3gMT^2}{6gT^2 - 48\pi^2 l}\right)^2$

Question 261:

Given a curve with the equation $y = 8 - 4x - 2x^2$ and a line $y = k(x + 4)$, find the values of k for which the line and the curve are tangent to each other.

A. $-4 < k \leq 4$

B. $k = 4, k = 20$

C. $4 < k < 20$

D. $k = -4, k = 4$

Question 262:

Consider the infinite series, $x - \left(\frac{1}{2}\right)x^2 + \left(\frac{1}{4}\right)x^3 - \left(\frac{1}{8}\right)x^4 \ldots$

Given that we know that the fifth term of the series is $\left(\frac{1}{32}\right)$, what is summation of the series given that the series converges as it heads toward infinity?

A. $\dfrac{16^{\frac{1}{5}}}{2 + \frac{(16^{\frac{1}{5}})}{2}}$

B. $\dfrac{1}{1 - (32)^{\frac{1}{4}}}$

C. $\dfrac{8^{\frac{1}{5}}}{1 + 8^{\frac{1}{5}}}$

D. $\dfrac{2}{2 - (16)^{\frac{1}{4}}}$

E. $\dfrac{-2}{2 + (16)^{\frac{1}{4}}}$

F. $\dfrac{1}{64 - 8^{\frac{1}{5}}}$

Question 263:

If $\log_2 3 . \log_3 4 . \log_4 5 \ldots \log_n(n + 1) \leq 10$, what is the largest value of n that satisfies this equation?

A. 1022
B. 824
C. 842
D. 1023
E. 1020
F. 890

Question 264:

a,b,c is a geometric progression where a,b,c are real numbers. If $a + b + c = 26$ and $a^2 + b^2 + c^2 = 364$, find b.

A. $3\sqrt{2}$
B. 6
C. $2\sqrt{6}$
D. 9
E. 4
F. $2\sqrt{3}$

Question 265:

Given that a>0, find the value of a for which the minimal value of the function $f(x) = (a^2 + 1)x^2 - 2ax + 10$ in the interval $x \in [0; 12]$ is $\frac{451}{50}$.

    A.   7

    B.   12

    C.   5

    D. $\frac{50}{125}$

    E.   8

    F.   10

Question 266:

If the probability that it will rain tomorrow is $\frac{2}{3}$ and the probability that it will rain and snow the following day is $\frac{1}{5}$, given that the probability of rain and snow occurring on any given day are independent from one another, what is the probability that it will snow the day after tomorrow?

    A. $\frac{10}{3}$

    B. $\frac{3}{10}$

    C. $\frac{2}{15}$

    D. $\frac{15}{2}$

    E. $\frac{4}{9}$

    F. $\frac{1}{5}$

Question 267:

If $\cos 2\theta = \frac{3}{4}$, then $\frac{1}{\cos^2\theta - \sin^2\theta} =$

    A. $\frac{4}{3}$

    B.   4

    C. -1

    D. $\frac{3}{4}$

    E.   2

    F.   1

Question 268:

Describe the geometrical transformation that maps the graph of $y = 0.2^x$ onto the graph of $y = 5^x$.

    A.   Reflection in the x-axis

    B.   Reflection in the y-axis

    C.   Multiplication by a scale factor of 25

    D.   Addition of the constant term 4.8

E. Multiplication by scale factor of 5

F. Multiplication by scale factor 1/25

Question 269:

Find the solution to the equation $\log_4(2x + 3) + \log_4(2x + 15) - 1 = \log_4(14x + 5)$

There is no solution

A. $\frac{2}{5}$

B. $\frac{5}{2}$

C. -1

D. 1

E. 0

Question 270:

Rearrange the following equation in terms of t: $x = \frac{\sqrt{b^3 - 9st}}{13j} + \int_{-z}^{z} 9a - 7$

A. $t = \frac{(13jx - \int_{-z}^{z} 9a - 7)^2 - b^3}{9s}$

B. $t = \frac{13jx^2}{b^3 - 9s} - \int_{-z}^{z} 9a - 7$

C. $t = x - \frac{\sqrt{b^3 - 9s}}{13j} - \int_{-z}^{z} 9a - 7$

D. $t = \frac{x^2}{\frac{b^3 - 9s}{13j} + \int_{-z}^{z} 9a - 7}$

E. $t = \frac{[13j(x - \int_{-z}^{z} 9a - 7)]^2 - b^3}{-9s}$

Question 271:

Simplify: $m = \sqrt{\frac{9xy^3z^5}{3x^9yz^4}} - m$

A. $m = \sqrt{\frac{3y^2z}{x^8}} - m$

B. $m^2 = \frac{3y^2z}{x^8} - m$

C. $2m = \sqrt{\frac{3y^2z}{x^8}}$

D. $2m^2 = 3x^{-8}y^2z$

E. $4m^2 = 3x^{-8}y^2z$

Question 272:

The normal to the curve $y = e^{2x-5}$ at the point $P(2, e^{-1})$ intersects the x-axis at the point A and the y-axis at the point B. Which of the following is an appropriate formula for the area of the triangle that is formed in terms of e, m, and n, where m and n are integers?

A. $\dfrac{(e^2+1)^m}{e^n}$

B. $\dfrac{(e^3+1)^{\frac{1}{n}}}{m}$

C. $\dfrac{e^n}{(e^2+1)^m}$

D. $\dfrac{m^{\frac{1}{n}}}{e^3+1}$

E. $\dfrac{e^{2m}}{e^n+1}$

F. $\dfrac{(e^2-1)^m}{e^{2n}}$

Question 273:

Given that $\sec x - \tan x = -5$, find the value of cos x.

A. -0.2

B. 0.2

C. $-\dfrac{13}{5}$

D. $\dfrac{-5}{13}$

E. 0.5

F. -0.5

Question 274:

Consider the line with equation $y = 2x + k$ where k is a constant, and the curve $y = x^2 + (3k - 4)x + 13$. Given that the line and the curve do not intersect, what are the possible values of k?

A. $-\dfrac{1}{3} < k < 3$

B. $-\dfrac{4}{9} < k < 4$

C. $\dfrac{1}{2} < k < \dfrac{5}{3}$

D. $\dfrac{3}{2} < k \le \dfrac{8}{3}$

E. $\dfrac{1}{3} < k < 3$

F. $-3 < k < \dfrac{1}{3}$

Question 275:

A circle with centre $C(5,-3)$ passes through $A(-2,1)$, and the point T lies on the tangent to the circle such that AT = 4. What is the length of the line CT?

  A. 9

  B. 18

  C. $\sqrt{95}$

  D. $8\sqrt{2}$

  E. $\sqrt{69}$

Question 276:

What is the equation of the quadratic function that passes through the x-coordinates of the stationary points of $y = x^2 e^x$?

  A. This quadratic function does not exist

  B. $x^2 + 2x$

  C. x^2

  D. $x^2 - 2x$

  E. $x^2 + 4x$

  F. $2x^2 - 1$

Question 277:

Which of the following equations is a correct simplification of the equation $\frac{x^2-16}{x^2-4x}$?

  A. $1 - \frac{4}{x}$

  B. $\frac{x+4}{x}$

  C. $\frac{x-4}{x}$

  D. $\frac{4}{x}$

  E. $\frac{x(x-4)}{x}$

  F. $\frac{x+4}{4x}$

Question 278:

A bag only contains 2n blue balls and n red balls. All the balls are identical apart from colour. One ball is randomly selected and not replaced. A second ball is then randomly selected. What is the probability that at least one of the selected balls is red?

  A. $\frac{4n}{3(3n-1)}$

  B. $\frac{5n-1}{3(3n-1)}$

  C. $\frac{5n-5}{3(3n-1)}$

  D. $\frac{4n-2}{3(3n-1)}$

E. $\frac{n-5}{9(n-1)}$

F. $\frac{4n-1}{3(3n-1)}$

Question 279:

For what values of the non-zero real number a does the equation $ax^2 + (a-2)x = 2$ have real and distinct roots?

A. $a \neq -2$

B. $a > 2$

C. $a > -2$

D. No values of a.

E. $a \neq 0$

F. $a > 5$

Question 280:

The sum of the roots of the equation $2^{2x} - 8 \times 2^x + 15 = 0$ is

A. 4

B. 16

C. $\log_{10}\left(\frac{15}{2}\right)$

D. $\frac{\log_{10} 15}{\log_{10} 2}$

E. 8

F. $\log_2\left(\frac{2}{3}\right)$

Question 281:

Given that $a^{3x}b^x c^{4x} = 2$, where a > 0, b > 0, and c > 0, then what does x equal?

A. $x = \frac{2}{3a+b+4c}$

B. $x = \frac{2}{(\log_{10} a^3 bc^4)}$

C. $x = \frac{\log_{10} 2}{\log_{10}(a^3 bc^4)}$

D. $x = \log_{10}\frac{2}{(ab^2c^3)}$

E. $x = \frac{\log_2 10}{\log_2(a^3 bc^4)}$

F. $x = \log_{10}\frac{2}{(a^3 bc^4)}$

Question 282:

The curve $y = x^2 + 3$ is reflected about the line $y = x$ and subsequently translated by the vector $\binom{4}{2}$. Which of the following is the x-intercept of the resulting curve?

A. -2

B. 11

C. 7

    D. -11

    E. 8

    F. -8

Question 283:

The vertex of an equilateral triangle is covered by a circle whose radius is half the height of the triangle. What percentage of the triangle is covered by the circle?

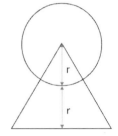

    A. 12%

    B. 16%

    C. 23%

    D. 33%

    E. 41%

    F. 50%

Question 284:

Three equal circles fit into a quadrilateral as shown, what is the height of the quadrilateral?

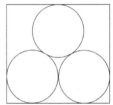

    A. $2\sqrt{3}r$

    B. $(2 + \sqrt{3})r$

    C. $(4 - \sqrt{3})r$

    D. $3r$

    E. $4r$

    F. More Information Needed

Question 285:

Two pyramids have equal volume and height, one with a square of side length **a** and one with a hexagonal base of side length **b**. What is the ratio of the side length of the bases?

    A. $\sqrt{\frac{3\sqrt{3}}{2}}$

    B. $\sqrt{\frac{2\sqrt{3}}{3}}$

    C. $\sqrt{\frac{3}{2}}$

    D. $\frac{2\sqrt{3}}{3}$

    E. $\frac{3\sqrt{3}}{2}$

Question 286:

One 9 cm cube is cut into 3 cm cubes. The total surface area increases by a factor of:

    A. $\frac{1}{3}$

    B. $\sqrt{3}$

    C. 3

D. 9

E. 27

Question 287:

A cone has height twice its base width (four times the circle radius). What is the cone angle (half the angle at the vertex)?

A. $30°$

B. $\sin^{-1}\left(\frac{r}{2}\right)$

C. $\sin^{-1}\left(\frac{1}{\sqrt{17}}\right)$

D. $\cos^{-1}(\sqrt{17})$

Question 288:

A hemispherical speedometer has a maximum speed of 200 mph. What is the angle travelled by the needle at a speed of 70 mph?

A. $28°$

B. $49°$

C. $63°$

D. $88°$

E. $92°$

Question 289:

Two rhombuses, A and B, are similar. The area of A is 10 times that of B. What is the ratio of the smallest angles over the ratio of the shortest sides?

A. 0

B. $\frac{1}{10}$

C. $\frac{1}{\sqrt{10}}$

D. $\sqrt{10}$

E. ∞

Question 290:

If $f^{-1}(-x) = \ln(2x^2)$ what is $f(x)$?

A. $\sqrt{\frac{e^y}{2}}$

B. $\sqrt{\frac{e^{-y}}{2}}$

C. $\frac{e^y}{2}$

D. $\frac{-e^y}{2}$

E. $\sqrt{\frac{e^y}{2}}$

Question 291:

Which of the following is largest for $0 < x < 1$

    A. $log_8(x)$
    B. $log_{10}(x)$
    C. e^x
    D. x^2
    E. $\sin(x)$

Question 292:

x is proportional to y cubed, y is proportional to the square root of z. $x \propto y^3, y \propto \sqrt{z}$.

If z doubles, x changes by a factor of:

    A. $\sqrt{2}$
    B. 2
    C. $2\sqrt{2}$
    D. $\sqrt[3]{4}$
    E. 4

Question 293:

The area between two concentric circles (shaded) is three times that of the inner circle.

What's the size of the gap?

    A. r
    B. $\sqrt{2}r$
    C. $\sqrt{3}r$
    D. $2r$
    E. $3r$
    F. $4r$

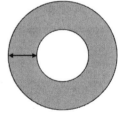

Question 294:

Solve $-x^2 \le 3x - 4$

    A. $x \ge \frac{4}{3}$
    B. $1 \le x \le 4$
    C. $x \le 2$
    D. $x \ge 1$ or $x \ge -4$
    E. $-1 \le x \le \frac{3}{4}$

Question 295:

The volume of a sphere is numerically equal to its projected area. What is its radius?

 A. $\frac{1}{2}$
 B. $\frac{2}{3}$
 C. $\frac{3}{4}$
 D. $\frac{4}{3}$
 E. $\frac{3}{2}$

Question 296:

What is the range where $x^2 < \frac{1}{x}$?

 A. $x < 0$
 B. $0 < x < 1$
 C. $x > 0$
 D. $x \geq 1$
 E. *None*

Question 297:

Simplify and solve: (e - a) (e + b) (e − c) (e + d) ...(e - z)?

 A. 0
 B. e^{26}
 C. e^{26} (a-b+c-d...+z)
 D. e^{26} (a+b-c+d...-z)
 E. e^{26} (abcd...z)
 F. None of the above.

Question 298:

Find the value of k such that the vectors $a = -i + 6j$ and $b = 2i + kj$ are perpendicular.

 A. -2
 B. $-\frac{1}{3}$
 C. $\frac{1}{3}$
 D. 2

Question 299:

What is the perpendicular distance between point **p** with position vector $4i + 5j$ and the line L given by vector equation $r = -3i + j + \lambda(i + 2j)$

 A. $2\sqrt{7}$
 B. $5\sqrt{2}$

C. $2\sqrt{5}$

D. $7\sqrt{2}$

Question 300:

Find k such that point $\begin{pmatrix} 2 \\ k \\ -7 \end{pmatrix}$ lies within the plane $r = \begin{pmatrix} 2 \\ 3 \\ -1 \end{pmatrix} + \lambda \begin{pmatrix} 4 \\ 1 \\ 0 \end{pmatrix} + \mu \begin{pmatrix} 2 \\ 1 \\ 3 \end{pmatrix}$

A. -2

B. -1

C. 0

D. 1

E. 2

Question 301:

What is the largest solution to $\sin(-2\theta) = 0.5$ for $\frac{\pi}{2} \le x \le 2\pi$?

A. $\frac{5\pi}{3}$

B. $\frac{4\pi}{3}$

C. $\frac{5\pi}{6}$

D. $\frac{7\pi}{6}$

E. $\frac{11\pi}{6}$

Question 302:

$\cos^4(x) - \sin^4(x) \equiv$

A. $cos(2x)$

B. $2\cos(x)$

C. $sin(2x)$

D. $sin(x)cos(x)$

E. $tan(x)$

Question 303:

How many real roots does $y = 2x^5 - 3x^4 + x^3 - 4x^2 - 6x + 4$ have?

A. 1

B. 2

C. 3

D. 4

E. 5

Question 304:

What is the sum of 8 terms, $\sum_1^8 u_n$, of an arithmetic progression with $u_1 = 2$ and $d = 3$.

    A. 15
    B. 82
    C. 100
    D. 184
    E. 282

Question 305:

What is the coefficient of the x^2 term in the binomial expansion of $(2 - x)^5$?

    A. -80
    B. -48
    C. 40
    D. 48
    E. 80

Question 306:

Given you have already thrown a 6, what is the probability of throwing three consecutive 6s using a fair die?

    A. $\frac{1}{216}$
    B. $\frac{1}{36}$
    C. $\frac{1}{6}$
    D. $\frac{1}{2}$
    E. 1

Question 307:

Three people, A, B and C play darts. The probability that they hit a bullseye are respectively $\frac{1}{5}, \frac{1}{4}, \frac{1}{3}$. What is the probability that at least two shots hit the bullseye?

    A. $\frac{1}{60}$
    B. $\frac{1}{30}$
    C. $\frac{1}{12}$
    D. $\frac{1}{6}$
    E. $\frac{3}{20}$

Question 308:

If probability of having blonde hair is 1 in 4, the probability of having brown eyes is 1 in 2 and the probability of having both is 1 in 8, what is the probability of having neither blonde hair nor brown eyes?

    A. $\frac{1}{2}$

    B. $\frac{3}{4}$

    C. $\frac{3}{8}$

    D. $\frac{5}{8}$

    E. $\frac{7}{8}$

Question 309:

Differentiate and simplify $y = x(x + 3)^4$

    A. $(x + 3)^3$

    B. $(x + 3)^4$

    C. $x(x + 3)^3$

    D. $(5x + 3)(x + 3)^3$

    E. $5x^3(x + 3)$

Question 310:

Evaluate $\int_1^2 \frac{2}{x^2}\,dx$

    A. -1

    B. $\frac{1}{3}$

    C. 1

    D. $\frac{21}{4}$

    E. 2

Question 311:

Express $\frac{5i}{1+2i}$ in the form $a + bi$

    A. $1 + 2i$

    B. $4i$

    C. $1 - 2i$

    D. $2 + i$

    E. $5 - i$

Question 312:

Simplify $7\log_a(2) - 3\log_a(12) + 5\log_a(3)$

    A. $log_{2a}(18)$

    B. $log_a(18)$

    C. $log_a(7)$

    D. $9log_a(17)$

    E. $-log_a(7)$

Question 313:

What is the equation of the asymptote of the function $y = \frac{2x^2 - x + 3}{x^2 + x - 2}$

- A. $x = 0$
- B. $x = 2$
- C. $y = 0.5$
- D. $y = 0$
- E. $y = 2$

Question 314:

Find the intersection(s) of the functions $y = e^x - 3$ and $y = 1 - 3e^{-x}$

- A. 0 and $\ln(3)$
- B. 1
- C. $\ln(4)$ and 1
- D. $\ln(3)$

Question 315:

Find the radius of the circle $x^2 + y^2 - 6x + 8y - 12 = 0$

- A. 3
- B. $\sqrt{13}$
- C. 5
- D. $\sqrt{37}$
- E. 12

Question 316:

What value of **a** minimises $\int_0^a 2\sin(-x)\,dx$?

- A. $0.5p$
- B. p
- C. $2p$
- D. $3p$
- E. 4

Question 317:

When $\frac{2x+3}{(x-2)(x-3)^2}$ is expressed as partial fractions, what is the numerator in the $\frac{A}{(x-2)}$ term:

- A. -7
- B. -1
- C. 3
- D. 6
- E. 7

END OF SECTION

Section 2

The Basics

In section 2, you have to write an essay based upon a passage. **There is no choice of essay title** meaning that you have to do the question that comes up. Whilst different questions will inevitably demand differing levels of comprehension and knowledge, it is important to realise that one of the major skills being tested is actually your ability to construct a logical and coherent argument- and to convey it to the lay-reader.

Section 2 of the ECAA is frequently neglected by lots of students, who choose to spend their time on section 1 instead. However, it is possible to rapidly improve in it and given that it may come up at your interview, well worth the time investment!

The aim of section 2 is not to write as much as you can. Rather, the examiner is looking for you to make interesting and well supported points, and tie everything neatly together for a strong conclusion. Make sure you're writing critically and concisely; not rambling on. **Irrelevant material can actually lower your score.**

Essay Structure

Basic Structure

ECAA Essays should follow the standard format of Introduction à Main Body à Conclusion.

The introduction should be the smallest portion of the essay (no more than one small paragraph) and be used to provide a smooth segue into the rather more demanding "argue for/against" part of the question. This main body requires a firm grasp of the concept being discussed and the ability to strengthen and support the argument with a wide variety of examples from multiple fields. This section should give a balanced approach to the question, exploring **at least two distinct ideas**. Supporting evidence should be provided throughout the essay, with examples referred to when possible.

The concluding final part effectively is a chance for you to shine- be brave and make an **innovative yet firmly grounded conclusion** for an exquisite mark. The conclusion should bring together all sides of the argument, in order to reach a clear and concise answer to the question. There should be an obvious logical structure to the essay, which reflects careful planning and preparation.

Paragraphs

Paragraphs are an important formatting tool which show that you have thought through your arguments and are able to structure your ideas clearly. A new paragraph should be used every time a new idea is introduced. There is no single correct way to arrange paragraphs, but it's important that each paragraph flows smoothly from the last. A slick, interconnected essay shows that you have the ability to communicate and organise your ideas effectively.

Remember- the emphasis should remain on quality and not quantity. An essay with fewer paragraphs, but with well-developed ideas, is much more effective than a number of short, unsubstantial paragraphs that fail to fully grasp the question at hand.

Planning

Why should I plan my essay?

The vast **majority of problems are caused by a lack of planning** - usually because students just want to get writing as they are worried about finishing on time. Fourty minutes is long enough to be able to plan your essay well and *still* have time to write it so don't feel pressured to immediately start writing.

There are multiple reasons you should plan your essay for the first 5-10 minutes of section 2:

- It allows you to get all your thoughts ready before you put pen to paper.
- You'll write faster once you have a plan.
- You run the risk of missing the point of the essay or only answering part of it if you don't plan adequately.

How much time should I plan for?

There is no set period of time that should be dedicated to planning, and everyone will dedicate a different length of time to the planning process. You should spend as long planning your essay as you require, but it is essential that you leave enough time to write the essay. As a rough guide, it is **worth spending about 5-10 minutes to plan** and the remaining time on writing the essay. However, this is not a strict rule, and you are advised to tailor your time management to suit your individual style.

How should I go about the planning process?

There are a variety of methods that can be employed in order to plan essays (e.g. bullet-points, mind-maps etc). If you don't already know what works best, it's a good idea to experiment with different methods.

Generally, the first step is to gather ideas relevant to the question, which will form the basic arguments around which the essay is to be built. You can then begin to structure your essay, including the way that points will be linked. At this stage it is worth considering the balance of your argument, and confirming that you have considered arguments from both sides of the debate. Once this general structure has been established, it is useful to consider any examples or real-world information that may help to support your arguments. Finally, you can begin to assess the plan as a whole, and establish what your conclusion will be based on your arguments.

Introduction

Why are introductions important?

An introduction provides tutors with their first opportunity to examine your work. The introduction is where first impressions are formed, and these can be extremely important in producing a convincing argument. A well-constructed introduction shows that you have really thought about the question, and can indicate the logical flow of arguments that is to come.

What should an introduction do?

A good introduction should **briefly explain the statement or quote** and give any relevant background information in a concise manner. However, don't fall into the trap of just repeating the statement in a different way. The introduction is the first opportunity to suggest an answer to the question posed- the main body is effectively your justification for this answer.

Main Body

How do I go about making a convincing point?

Each idea that you propose should be supported and justified, in order to build a convincing overall argument. A point can be solidified through a basic Point à Evidence à Evaluation process. By following this process, you can be assured each sentence within a paragraph builds upon the last, and that all the ideas presented are well solidified.

How do I achieve a logical flow between ideas?

One of the most effective ways of displaying a good understanding of the question is to keep a logical flow throughout your essay. This means linking points effectively between paragraphs, and creating a congruent train of thought for the examiner as the argument develops. A good way to generate this flow of ideas is to provide ongoing comparisons of arguments, and discussing whether points support or dispute one another.

Should I use examples?

In short – yes! Examples can help boost the validity of arguments, and can help display high quality writing skills. Examples can add a lot of weight to your argument and make an essay much more relevant to the reader. When using examples, you should ensure that they are relevant to the point being made, as they will not help to support an argument if they are not.

Some questions will provide more opportunities to include examples than others so don't worry if you aren't able to use as many examples as you would have liked. There is no set rule about how many examples should be included!

> ***Top tip!*** Remember that there is no single correct answer to these questions and you're not expected to be able to fit everything onto one page. Instead it's better to pick a few key points to focus on.

Conclusion

The conclusion provides an opportunity to emphasise the **overall sentiment of your essay** which readers can then take away. It should summarise what has been discussed during the main body and give a definitive answer to the question.

Some students use the conclusion to **introduce a new idea that hasn't been discussed**. This can be an interesting addition to an essay, and can help make you stand out. However, it is by no means, a necessity. In fact, a well-organised, 'standard' conclusion is likely to be more effective than an adventurous but poorly executed one.

Common Mistakes

Ignoring the other side of the argument

You need to ensure that you show an appreciation for the fact that there are often two sides to the argument. Where appropriate, you should outline both points of view and how they pertain to the essay's main principles and then come to a reasoned judgement.

A good way to do this is to propose an argument that might be used against you, and then to argue why it doesn't hold true or seem relevant. You may use the format: *"some may say that…but this doesn't seem to be important because…"* in order to dispel opposition arguments, whilst still displaying that you have considered them. For example, *"some may say that fox hunting shouldn't be banned because it is a tradition. However, witch hunting was also once a tradition – we must move on with the times".*

Missing Topic Sentences

A reader who is pressed for time should be able to read your introduction, the first line of every paragraph and your conclusion and be able to follow your argument. The filling of a paragraph will elaborate your point with examples. But the first sentence of the paragraph should provide the headline point.

- Use topic sentences as punchy summaries for the theme of each paragraph
- Include a clear summary of the structure of your essay in your introduction
- Summarize briefly the theme of your points in your conclusion
- Ensure your conclusion also tells the reader your final decision

Undefined Terms

Debates can be won or lost on the basis of the interpretation of a key term; ensure your interpretation of the key words is clearly explained. For example: "Does science or art shape our world?" Here, your interpretation of what it means to *shape* something is absolutely crucial to lay out before you start writing, so that your reader knows the scope of your argument. If *shape* to you means invent something new (like a potter shaping a pot out of a lump of clay), state this. But if you interpret *shape* to mean a gentle guide or influence on something, state that. You can then be more focused and precise in your discussion. Likewise, for this title ensure you are clear about the scope of what is science and what is art.

- Define the key terms within the particular context of the question
- Be clear about your understanding of the scope

No Sign-Posting

There is a delight to enjoying a long journey if you know (1) where you are going, (2) what you will see on the way and (3) how long it will take to get there. For the reader of your essay, the same logic applies. State briefly but clearly in the final sentence of your introduction the topics you will cover (preferably in the order you will cover them!). You don't need to give the entire game away (don't necessarily tell your reader precisely what your 'wow-factor' will be) but you can give them a solid hint as to your final destination. For example, "Having discussed these arguments in favour and against fox hunting, we conclude with a consideration of the wider issue of the role of governmental institutions in condoning and condemning the traditional pursuits of citizens." It is sometimes tempting to try to surprise your reader with an unexpected twist but this is not best practice for an academic essay.

- Don't surprise your reader with unexpected twists in the main essay
- Do be clear in your introduction about the number of points you will make
- Do include your points in the order they will appear

Long Introductions

Some students can start rambling and make introductions too long and unfocussed. Although background information about the topic can be useful, it is normally not necessary. Instead, the **emphasis should be placed on responding to the question**. Some students also just **rephrase the question** rather than actually explaining it. The examiner knows what the question is, and repeating it in the introduction is simply a waste of space in an essay where you are limited to just one A4 side.

Not including a Conclusion

An essay that lacks a conclusion is incomplete and can signal that the answer has not been considered carefully or that your organisation skills are lacking. **The conclusion should be a distinct paragraph** in its own right and not just a couple of rushed lines at the end of the essay.

Sitting on the Fence

Students sometimes don't reach a clear conclusion. You need to **ensure that you give a decisive answer to the question** and clearly explain how you've reached this judgement. Essays that do not come to a clear conclusion generally have a smaller impact and score lower.

Conclusions with no 'Wow-Factor'

Try to 'zoom out' in your conclusion, rather than merely summarising the points you have made and deciding that one set outweighs the other. Put the question back in a wider context, so that your decision has a wow-factor for why it really matters. For instance, if you have answered the question, "Is world peace achievable?" and you think it isn't, say why this matter. For example: "In an age of nuclear capability, attempts to achieve the impossible is a waste of scarce resources, so we'd be better off focusing policy and diplomacy on building safety nets to prevent escalations of inevitable conflicts into another world war."

- Don't only repeat your arguments again in your conclusion
- Don't sit on the fence in your conclusion
- Do use the conclusion to zoom out for the final punchline: why does this matter?

Missing the Point

Ensure you have identified what you think the 'Turning Point' of the question is, before you start writing. Within the title, which may be long and literary, identify the single core issue for you that you will discuss. For example, with the question, "Has the "digital age" destroyed the human right to anonymity?", restate it as a simple statement: the key question is whether previous to the introduction of digital technology we had a human right to anonymity which has now disappeared. You can then anchor your argument clearly on whether such a right had always existed before (perhaps so, perhaps not) and whether it has now disappeared (if it ever existed). By restating the key question, you will auto-generate a clear structure for yourself to follow.

- Work out the hinge of the question before you start writing and state it clearly

Worked Essay Questions

Passage 1

In 1972, the teenage king of Bhutan, Jigme Singye Wangchuck, declared that "gross national happiness is more important than gross domestic product". The sound bite has been echoed approvingly down the years, although the king may just have been making excuses. Bhutanese GDP per person was then the grinding poverty of about a dollar a day. If I were king of such a country, I'd be tempted to change the subject, too.

Clearly he had a point. Most of us would rather be poor and happy than rich and depressed. If so, gross national happiness seems a fine goal. But it is one thing for a monarch to announce that happiness is important. It's quite another to make people happy. Shangri-La does not move from fiction to reality just because we desire it.

Bhutan has not always lived up to its own hype. Same-sex intercourse is illegal, which suggests a country with a less-than-expansive view of whose happiness matters. Three decades ago, around 100,000 of the Nepali-speaking Lhotshampa minority fled Bhutan to escape military persecution during a campaign of ethnic cleansing on a colossal scale. One-sixth of the entire population of Bhutan ended up in refugee camps in Nepal.

Even setting aside this enormity, it's hard to see that Bhutan paid much more than lip service to gross national happiness. They hosted conferences, but according to a recent IMF working paper, nobody in the government collected systematic indicators on happiness until 2005. The World Happiness Report ranks Bhutan at 97th out of 156 countries, down from 84th a few years ago. Happiness is easy to venerate, but hard to generate, and even harder to measure.

Consider some of the issues that are notoriously bypassed by GDP, the most common measure of economic activity: digital services are hard to value, while by design GDP omits any consideration of inequality or environmental damage. Unpaid work — of which men do a great deal, and women a great deal more — is also left out.

But if our aim is (for example) to reduce carbon emissions, we don't achieve it by moaning about GDP. We achieve it with specific policies such as carbon taxes and investments in public transport and a renewable-friendly electric grid. Neither gender equality nor respect for unpaid work would be automatically improved by any change in the way national income accounts are computed.

The specifics matter when it comes to happiness, too. Broad research into the causes of national happiness has tended to produce banal conclusions: we tend to compare ourselves to others, unemployment makes us miserable, and we hate being ill. There is nothing here to suggest that we need to overhaul commonplace policies such as redistributive taxation, the avoidance of recessions, and support for public health.

Just as with GDP itself, it is only when we move to the specifics that gross national happiness becomes useful. Richard Layard, one of the leading happiness researchers, argues that mental illness is a leading cause of misery, and that it can be treated very cost-effectively. That seems useful enough to me, but that doesn't seem to require economists' focus to realise.

Question

"Economists should be more concerned with happiness and wellbeing than GDP."
Discuss with reference to the passage above.

Example Plan

Introduction: Set the scene...

- Define "concerned with". This could mean "focus on..." or "worried about". Here I take it here to mean a that latter because it allows for a more expansive essay, however either would be appropriate given context.
- The key question to be answered is therefore: Should economic analysis and policies be focussed on improving a nation's happiness, instead of conventional measures of wealth and prosperity?

Paragraph 1: Just because it's better doesn't make it the focus...

- Traditionally economic analysis and economic policies have been focussed on promoting economic growth conventionally measured through GDP per capita. The article makes the assertion that "many of us would rather be poor and happy, than rich and miserable".
- On this logic, economists and the policies they devise to help governments, should be focussed on generating happiness for people rather than wealth.
- Yet this assumes that economists and their policies should be focussed on outcomes that are most desirable, without paying attention to pragmatics.

Paragraph 2: Challenge 1 – It isn't pragmatic to be concerned with happiness...

- One reason for economists remaining focussed on GDP is that it isn't pragmatic to be focussed on the alternative; namely happiness and wellbeing.
- Happiness is notoriously hard to measure. As the article explains generic measures of happiness are subject to the same criticisms as GDP (see paragraph 7 in the article).
- Equally it is not clear that happiness is the same for every person. Whilst wealth is somewhat consistent across individuals e.g. more money and better-quality stuff = more wealth; it is not clear that what makes me happy makes any other individual happy. In a world where policy is general and impacts all, economists cannot aim to please everyone.

Paragraph 3: It isn't right to be concerned with happiness...

- This all assumes thus far that happiness is what economists **should** be concerned about if only it were possible to measure and practical to increase.
- However, GDP has a lot going for it, indeed it has remained the headline measure for the IMF even for Bhutan for much of the last few decades (paragraph 4).
- The criticism of GDP in paragraph 5, makes a compelling case against it's general nature, but whilst it advocates for measuring specifics, it does not say that national income (GDP) is the wrong measure entirely.
- Indeed, measuring wealth/national income is crucially important – without it public services cannot be provided, a country struggles to trade for things it needs and it's people have limited access to resources, capital or goods that are required for living a reasonable quality of life.
- There is therefore a compelling argument for national income/GDP to remain the concern of economists for both analysis and policy purposes.

Conclusion

- Summarize the points:
    - o The article seems to suggest at points that happiness should be the concern of economists, above GDP and that it should be considered with specificity to be useful to economists.
- Having decided in this plan to argue against the statement summarise your three points:
    - o Take the assertion that happiness is more important than GDP to be right however this isn't enough to suggest that it should be the primary concern of economists.
    - o It isn't pragmatic to be concerned with happiness and therefore it shouldn't be the primary concern
    - o It isn't even right to be concerned with happiness anyway.
- Zoom out and say why the question really matters and conclude.

Passage 2

THE annual labour of every nation is the fund which originally supplies it with all the necessaries and conveniences of life which it annually consumes, and which consist always either in the immediate produce of that labour, or in what is purchased with that produce from other nations.

According therefore as this produce, or what is purchased with it, bears a greater or smaller proportion to the number of those who are to consume it, the nation will be better or worse supplied with all the necessaries and conveniences for which it has occasion.

But this proportion must in every nation be regulated by two different circumstances; first, by the skill, dexterity, and judgment with which its labour is generally applied; and, secondly, by the proportion between the number of those who are employed in useful labour, and that of those who are not so employed. Whatever be the soil, climate, or extent of territory of any nation, the abundance or scantiness of its annual supply must, in that particular situation, depend upon those two circumstances.

The abundance or scantiness of this supply, too, seems to depend more upon the former of those two circumstances than upon the latter. Among the savage nations of hunters and fishers, every individual who is able to work, is more or less employed in useful labour, and endeavours to provide, as well as he can, the necessaries and conveniences of life, for himself, or such of his family or tribe as are either too old, or too young, or too infirm to go a hunting and fishing. Such nations, however, are so miserably poor that, from mere want, they are frequently reduced, or, at least, think themselves reduced, to the necessity sometimes of directly destroying, and sometimes of abandoning their infants, their old people, and those afflicted with lingering diseases, to perish with hunger, or to be devoured by wild beasts. Among civilised and thriving nations, on the contrary, though a great number of people do not labour at all, many of whom consume the produce of ten times, frequently of a hundred times more labour than the greater part of those who work; yet the produce of the whole labour of the society is so great that all are often abundantly supplied, and a workman, even of the lowest and poorest order, if he is frugal and industrious, may enjoy a greater share of the necessaries and conveniences of life than it is possible for any savage to acquire

(Adam Smith, Wealth of Nations)

Question

"What is Adam Smith argument in the passage. Do you agree or disagree? (Use examples from modern economics)
Discuss with reference to the passage above.

Example Plan

Introduction: What is Adam Smith's Argument in the passage?

- Smith's argument can essentially be deconstructed as follows:
    - Refer first to Para 3 where he explains that the proportion that is produced in a country versus the population (GDP per capita) will be determined by the application of labour and the number of people employed. This goes against an argument that soil, climate, geography of the nation can influence the economic wealth of that country.
    - Smith then goes on to claim in paragraph 4 that wealth in fact whilst dependent on both factors, depends on the former of the two more than the latter; that production is about skill not number of worker. He claims nations that are poor are often at full employment but do not work with skill. In a wealthy society however, it is often the case that individuals are not all employed, but the production of a few well employed is so great to as provide for all.

Paragraph 1: Adam Smith's logic does seem to apply to modern countries?

- Smith is arguing that the reason countries have become wealthy is because they apply labour with more precision, and have more skilled labour.
- Take the cadre of modern day developed economies: they are not the most populous countries in the world e.g. UK, Japan, European countries are all some of the most developed. They do however all have developed industries (service orientated or high-skilled manufacturing economies with highly skilled labour forces). Additionally, they do also have higher rates of unemployment.
- This all seems to validate Smith's argument that it matters not the rate of employment but rather the skill of the employed that drive economic prosperity.
- Expand with examples of your own e.g. UK development in 80s and 90s, rise of Japan and the Far-East as skilled labour economies for hi-tech manufacturing (Sony, Samsung etc…)

Paragraph 2: Employing lots of people hasn't seemed to drive wealth.

- Adam Smith make's a coherent argument for population size and even employment rates not being a significant contributing factor to the wealth of a nation. In fact, he suggests that you have historically seen many societies where all employable individual's (health and age dependent) work but are savage and primitive.
- Whilst extreme, there is validation for Adam Smith's logic in modern day examples. Possible examples include Asian economies where numerous individuals (young, old, infirm and those who can work) are employed in low wage jobs such as sweat shops etc… other examples could be rural economies in Africa.
- The economies whilst at full employment do not reap the rewards of their labour, the lack of high skilled individuals to develop high value products means that the majority of the valuable assets are owned or traded overseas.

Paragraph 3: However, Adam Smith ignores key factors that influence growth in a globalised world.

- Some could argue that Adam Smith's argument no longer applies in today's globalised world.
- Today when economies are integrated it could be no longer argued that wealth need be driven by internal processes, instead the ways in which a country is linked with, and to whom, can be said to drive growth and wealth.
- Take for example some of the countries in Africa where it is shown that post-colonial connections to their former colonial power, are correlated with wealth because of trade links. This has nothing to do with labour etc…

Conclusion

- Summarize the points:
  - Adam Smith's argument does seem to reflect the economic facts we see in the modern world.
    - This applies in terms of the precise application of skilled labour
    - It also appears to apply in the idea that large populations and close to full employment does not drive economic wealth.
- Zoom out and say why the question really matters (give your essay the 'wow-factor'):
  - Important to understand for policy decisions in terms of driving economic growth: to drive a wealthy economy policy should focus on training and skills development, rather than getting everyone to full employment. However, it should be noted that this relies on strong redistribution as wealth can then become concentrated.

Passage 3 – Animal Spirits

Even apart from the instability due to speculation, there is the instability due to the characteristic of human nature that a large proportion of our positive activities depend on spontaneous optimism rather than on a mathematical expectation, whether moral or hedonistic or economic. Most, probably, of our decisions to do something positive, the full consequences of which will be drawn out over many days to come, can only be taken as a result of animal spirits—of a spontaneous urge to action rather than inaction, and not as the outcome of a weighted average of quantitative benefits multiplied by quantitative probabilities. Enterprise only pretends to itself to be mainly actuated by the statements in its own prospectus, however candid and sincere. Only a little more than an expedition to the South Pole, is it based on an exact calculation of benefits to come. Thus if the animal spirits are dimmed and the spontaneous optimism falters, leaving us to depend on nothing but a mathematical expectation, enterprise will fade and die; —though fears of loss may have a basis no more reasonable than hopes of profit had before.

It is safe to say that enterprise which depends on hopes stretching into the future benefits the community as a whole. But individual initiative will only be adequate when reasonable calculation is supplemented and supported by animal spirits, so that the thought of ultimate loss which often overtakes pioneers, as experience undoubtedly tells us and them, is put aside as a healthy man puts aside the expectation of death.

This means, unfortunately, not only that slumps and depressions are exaggerated in degree, but that economic prosperity is excessively dependent on a political and social atmosphere which is congenial to the average business man.

(John Maynard Keynes)

Question

What does Keynes mean by "Animal Spirits"? What are the implications, if true, for current economic policy? (Discuss with examples).

Example Plan

Introduction

- Animal Spirits according to Keynes are the "spontaneous urge to action rather than inaction, and not as the outcome of a weighted average of quantitative benefits multiplied by quantitative probabilities".
- By this Keynes means that despite the economic assumption of rationality, a great deal of decision making is dependent upon unexplained or spontaneous feelings by humans; those animal spirits that exist within us all.
- Keynes sees animal spirits as that part of us all that emotionally drives our decision making either by instilling confidence or fear and as such, "economic prosperity is excessively dependent the political and social atmosphere".

Paragraph 1: Implication for economic policy 1 – Policy based on assumptions of rationality can sometimes not have the desired impact

- One of the major implications for economic policy of animal spirits is that when economic policy is implemented then the consequences are often unpredictable.
- For example: at this point you could use any example but below is an example

- Expansionary Fiscal policy: e.g. monetary spending or tax cuts/breaks. The intention of this policy is to increase disposable income with the intention of increasing consumption and investment, yielding economic growth. However, animal spirits suggest that whilst theoretically, a rational individual would act in accordance with a rational analysis of the benefits from spending increases, in fact their propensity to spend is highly dependent on animal spirits in the form of confidence, trust and other emotions that could induce spending decisions.
- This would then lead into the next implication – that governments should try and influence animal spirits.

Paragraph 2: Implication for policy 2 – Policy should sometimes aim to impact animal spirits

- To ensure the effectiveness of economic policies enacted by governments, they should sometimes try to impact animal spirits, or at least not neglect them.
- Why? The government cannot neglect animal spirits because they are so influential. Therefore, in making decisions around policy the government should consider the impact they can have on these sentiments e.g. confidence, trust etc…
- Examples for this could include scheduling of events such as forecasts and economic announcements, central bank messaging, statements to the media, geo-political events and their handling, elections, wars and other national social events.

Paragraph 3: Implication for policy 3 – Recessions can be unpredictable

- Another major implication stemming from the concept of animal spirits, is its consequences for the unpredictable nature of certain events.
- For example, stories of corruption and broken trust can reduce confidence, and that can greatly contribute to economic depressions and confidence being undermined can lead to crisis. Possible examples include:
  - Stories – humans get behind stories and can be positive. E.g. is story of the internet and a new era of tech fuelled one of history's biggest stock market bubbles in the early 2000s. Similarly, during the depression in the US in the 1890s the run on the banks was caused by stories spread of corruption and fragility in the financial system, when in fact many were untrue.
  - In the 1980s crisis ensued when moral hazard undermined confidence; savings and loan entrepreneurs made risky investments knowing that the government would rescue them – similar example in 2008 Sub-Prime Mortgage crisis. Erosion of confidence from this in some cases sparked and certainly deepened the recessions.
- This is worrying for policy makers because it seems to imply that there are some factors that are simply out of their control. (At this point you could introduce an argument in defence of policy makers which suggests that since they cannot control animal spirits perhaps they need to be wholly reactive etc…).

Conclusion

- Summarize the points:
  - Animal Spirits can distort the theoretically predicted impact of economic policies which are based on the assumptions of rationality
  - A second implication for policy makers is that they should sometime not only account for, but aim to influence animal spirits using communications or timings of events.
  - A third implication of animal spirits is that they render economic events such as recessions somewhat unpredictable.

- Likely conclusion is that clearly animal spirits hold great implications of economic policy makers in a variety of ways; including potentially very negative and therefore cannot be ignored and must be accounted for as much as possible.

Passage 4

Most institutions in the country are businesses – shops, factories, energy companies, airlines, and train companies, to name a few types. They are the bedrock of society, employ most people in it and it is, thus, crucial that we examine their values.

The overriding objective of businesses is to make the most profit (i.e. maximise on revenue and minimise on costs). The notion was first popularly expounded by Adam Smith in his book, 'The Wealth of Nations' in 1776. Furthermore, his view was that if an individual considers merely their own interests to create and sell goods or services for the most profit, the invisible hand of the market will lead that activity to maximise the welfare of society. For example, in order to maximise profits, sellers will only produce and sell goods that society wants. If they try to sell things people don't want, no one would buy it. This is how the free market works. Indeed, the focus on profit is the basis on which companies operate and encourages them to innovate and produce goods that consumers want, such as iPhones and computers. So there are clear benefits to the profit maximisation theory.

This is a more effective society than, for example, a communist society where the government decides what to produce – as the government has no accurate way of deciding what consumers need and want. Arguably, the poverty that communist regimes such as the Soviet Union created have instilled this notion further.

However, were companies left to their own devices to engage in profit maximisation, what would stop them from exploiting workers? What would stop them from dumping toxic chemicals into public rivers? Engaging in such practices would reduce their costs of production, which would increase their profits. However, this would be very damaging to the environment. Accordingly, other objectives should be relevant. Businesses can also do other bad things to make a profit as well. For example, selling products to people who don't want or need them.

Corporate social responsibility entails other possible objectives for businesses, such as a consideration of the interests of stakeholders. A stakeholder is, in essence, anyone who is significantly affected by a company decision, such as employees or the local community. One business decision can have huge impacts on stakeholders. For example, a decision to transfer a call centre from the UK to India would likely increase profits, as wage costs for Indian workers can be much lower than that of British workers. This increase in profits would benefit the shareholders, however, it negatively harms other stakeholders. It would make many employees redundant. Here, there is arguably a direct conflict between profit maximisation and employees' interest. Nonetheless, moving call centres abroad does not always work. Given the different cultures and accents, companies have received complaints from frustrated customers. This, in fact, led BT to bring back a number of call centres to the UK.

However, the objective of profit maximisation has not always led to maximum welfare for society. Arguably, as banks sought to maximise their profits, they lent money to individuals who could not afford to pay it back. Eventually, many borrowers stopped meeting their repayments and lost banks enormous amounts. This led to a need for banks to be bailed out by the government and Lehman Brothers; one of the largest US banks that collapsed. Arguably, though, this was more due to idiocy rather than profit maximisation alone – in the end, the banks lost billions.

Question

"Enforcing Corporate Social Responsibility interferes with the market's ability to give people what they want." Discuss with reference to the passage above.

Example Plan

Introduction:

- Define Corporate Social Responsibility (from the passage). The market: here, we mean the goods and services offered for sale by businesses and bought by consumers. People: here we mean both the consumers in the market and those not participating in the market.
- The key question: If businesses are driven by the objective to maximise profits, does the market truly give people what they want?

Paragraph 1:

- Adam Smith's invisible hand tells us that the market will allocate resources to maximise the welfare of society. If goods were produced and not demanded, this would waste resources. This cannot happen as the resources used to make these goods would be allocated to make other, demanded, goods.
- *Passage Example:* "Sellers will only produce and sell goods that society wants." The businesses may be maximising profits, but they can only do so within the constraints of selling items that are wanted by the people. Thus, what is on offer in a market is determined by the people's wants.

Paragraph 2:

- We need Corporate Social Responsibility to prevent the profit maximisation of businesses affecting stakeholders who are not necessarily the direct consumer of the good or service being produced. Their loss may outweigh the gains of those engaged in the transaction and so we have a net loss,
- *Passage Example*: "Corporate social responsibility entails other possible objectives for businesses, such as consideration of the interests of stakeholders."

Paragraph 3:

- The problem here is not the functioning of the market, but instead all the people not fully understanding the impact of their consumption: with full information, people's wants will be satisfied by the market,
- *Passage Example:* "Dumping toxic chemicals into public rivers… would be very damaging to the environment." If the pollution is common knowledge, and if the majority of people think it is bad, they will buy goods from an alternative green business, and the polluting company will go out of business.
- *Passage Example:* "A decision to transfer a call centre from the UK to India … would make many employees redundant." If this is common knowledge the majority will switch their consumption to another business; indeed, we see BT had to relocate back to the UK to re-cooperate customers.

Paragraph 4:

- It may not be possible to fully inform customers, in which case the argument for regulation enforcing business responsibility is clear: external referees are needed to identify the good which is preferred for people and ensure they get the right one in the market.
- *Passage Example*: "Many borrowers stopped meeting their repayments…" Borrowers bought loans that were not fully understood by the players in the market and were too risky.

Conclusion

- Summarize the points:
    - Allocation is determined by people's demand: any interferences undermine people's wants.
    - Allocations may affect other stakeholders resulting in net-loss of welfare.
    - If all stakeholders (consumers, businesses and externally affected people) understand all the repercussions of production, wants will be satisfied directly in the market.
    - Full information for everyone is not feasible in some contexts.
- Now decide for yourself one way or another...
- Zoom out and say why the question really matters (just pick one to give your essay the 'wow-factor'):
- Government Intervention is needed to ensure market interactions are net-beneficial to society, not just to the active buyers and sellers. CSR gives a voice to the wants of the silent victims of markets.

Passage 5

"What are the rules which men naturally observe in exchanging them [goods] for money or for one another, I shall now proceed to examine. These rules determine what may be called the relative or exchangeable value of goods. The word 'Value', it is to be observed, has two different meanings, and sometimes expresses the utility of some particular object, and sometimes the power of purchasing other goods which the possession of that object conveys. The one may be called "value in use;" the other, "value in exchange." The things which have the greatest value in use have frequently little or no value in exchange; on the contrary, those which have the greatest value in exchange have frequently little or no value in use. Nothing is more useful than water: but it will purchase scarcely anything; scarcely anything can be had in exchange for it. A diamond, on the contrary, has scarcely any use-value; but a very great quantity of other goods may frequently be had in exchange for it."

(Adam Smith, Wealth of Nations)

This passage articulates a paradox in economics knows as the Paradox of Value or Diamond-Water Paradox. Smith noted that, even though life cannot exist without water and can easily exist without diamonds, diamonds are, pound for pound, vastly more valuable than water.

In a further passage Smith explains: "The real price of every thing, what every thing really costs to the man who wants to acquire it, is the toil and trouble of acquiring it."

(Adam Smith, Wealth of Nations)

Thus, Smith's explanation was the labour theory of value. This theory stated that the price of a good reflected the amount of labour and resources required to bring it to market. Smith believed diamonds were more expensive than water because they were more difficult to bring to market. Price on this view was related to a factor of production (namely, labour) and not to the point of view of the consumer (in which case there would be a relationship between price and utility.

Question

How convincing is Smith's explanation of Labour Theory of Value as a resolution of the 'Diamond-Water Paradox'? What other explanations are there, and are they more convincing?

Example Plan

Introduction:

- Introduce and summarize Smith's problem: simply that despite their differing values to humans, with water being integral to life and diamonds a superficial luxury diamonds hold far more value.
- Smith explains this by suggesting that the reason for this is because the value of a good is related to the labour involved in it production.
- State the structure of the essay and you likely conclusion since this is an argumentative piece.

Paragraph 1: The Labour Theory of Value

- Start by assessing the Labour Theory of Value as a convincing argument for resolving the Diamond-Water Paradox.

- On the one hand this seems logical because products which take a lot of skill to produce, or a lot of time will often cost more. E.g. for something with high production costs (directly related to the labour) such as an iPhone which must be designed, produced and shipped.
- However, labour theory of value struggles when trying to explain the price attached to good which have little or no production process or value. For example consider a perfectly formed gemstone found on a path, which would not have a lower market price than one which is produced artificially through significant labour or even one which has been mined and cut and polished through hard work.

Paragraph 2: Subjective Value – the opposite of Labour Theory seems more likely

- Another argument against the validity of the Labour theory of value is that it is not the case that costs and labour drive price, in fact price drives labour and cost.
- Consider goods that have high value such as fine wine, which is not valuable because it derives from expensive land and is produced by highly paid workers who exert effort. In fact, the price seems more likely to be the driver of the costs, because the product is valuable, the means of production are valuable.
- This suggests that the value of a product lies in the value people attach to it; so for a solution to this paradox we must look to why people value diamonds more than water.

Paragraph 3: Alternative 1 – Scarcity: Supply and Demand

- One clear alternative way of solving the argument lies in the relative rarity of the products then.
- Diamonds are rarer and therefore utility from a single diamond, is more valuable demand outstrips supply by a greater amount, than with water which is in abundant supply, thereby driving the price up.
- This is simple demand and supply, but can be countered by the following logic: Whilst it is true that supply of diamonds is much lower, it is not clear why demand would be the same. Indeed, it seems likely that demand for water is much higher than that of diamonds, water is more essential for life and has more uses.

Paragraph 4: Alternative 2 – Scarcity: marginal Utility

- The alternative means of solving this paradox lie in the theory of marginal utility; which suggests that the price of a good is derived from its most important use – namely that the price is determined by the usefulness of each unit of a good not the total utility of a good.
- Since diamonds are rarer, it is likely that they are put to their most important use thereby holding greater value. Since water is so abundant, each additional unit of water that becomes available can be applied to less urgent uses as more urgent uses for water are satisfied.
- Under this logic, any unit of water becomes less valuable because it is put to less and less valuable use. Conversely each unit of diamond is more valuable because it is in less supply so put to more use. One additional diamond is worth more than one additional glass of water for example.
- A further example for this logic comes from considering a man in a desert who would have greater marginal use for water than for diamonds, so water would hold more value for him, due to scarcity.

Conclusion

- Summarize the points:
    - Adam Smith solves the paradox with the labour theory of value
    - There is an opposite argument: subjective theory of value which yields two alternatives
    - Supply and Demand simply drives the higher price

- ○ The answer lies in the different marginal utilities of the goods due to their scarcity
- Give your answer as to which is more convincing backing it up with either logical reasoning or persuasive examples.
- Zoom out and say why this is important – fundamentally important question about value of goods and services. Important to consider how prices of these essential, yet currently abundant goods, may change as they become more scarce e.g. fossil fuels, clean water etc…

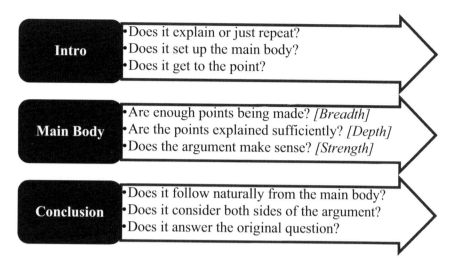

Final Advice

- ✓ Always answer the question clearly – this is the key thing examiner look for in an essay.
- ✓ Analyse each argument made, justifying or dismissing with logical reasoning.
- ✓ Keep an eye on the time/space available – an incomplete essay may be taken as a sign of a candidate with poor organisational skills.
- ✓ Ensure each paragraph has a new theme that is clearly differentiated from the previous one (don't just use a new paragraph to break your text up)
- ✓ Leave yourself time to write a conclusion – however short – that tells your reader which side of the fence you're on
- ✓ Do plan your essay before you start writing even the introduction; don't be tempted to dive straight into it
- ✓ Use pre-existing knowledge when possible – examples and real world data can be a great way to strengthen an argument- but don't make up statistics!
- ✓ Present ideas in a neat, logical fashion (easier for an examiner to absorb).
- ✓ Complete some practice questions in advance, in order to best establish your personal approach to the paper (particularly timings, how you plan etc.).

- ✗ Attempt to answer a question that you don't fully understand, or ignore part of a question.
- ✗ Rush or attempt to use too many arguments – it is much better to have fewer, more substantial points.
- ✗ Attempt to be too clever, or present false knowledge to support an argument – a tutor may call out incorrect facts etc.
- ✗ Panic if you don't know the answer the examiner wants – there is no right answer, the essay is not a test of knowledge but a chance to display reasoning skill. Start by defining the words in the question to get your mind thinking about ways to approach it
- ✗ Leave an essay unfinished – if time/space is short, wrap up the essay early in order to provide a conclusive response to the question. If you've only got a couple of minutes left, summarize your remaining points in a short bullet point each; these bullets contain just the topic sentence and (optionally) a quote from the passage to illustrate your point

Answers

Answer Key

Q	A	Q	A	Q	A	Q	A	Q	A	Q	A	Q	A
1	B	51	D	101	B	151	C	201	D	251	C	301	E
2	C	52	D	102	F	152	D	202	B	252	C	302	A
3	C	53	B	103	D	153	C	203	D	253	D	303	C
4	C	54	E	104	D	154	A	204	E	254	D	304	C
5	E	55	E	105	E	155	B	205	D	255	D	305	E
6	A	56	B	106	B	156	D	206	C	256	A	306	A
7	C	57	C	107	C	157	D	207	F	257	C	307	D
8	E	58	A	108	E	158	D	208	C	258	D	308	C
9	E	59	C	109	C	159	C	209	C	259	D	309	D
10	C	60	B	110	D	160	B	210	B	260	B	310	A
11	E	61	B	111	B	161	B	211	E	261	B	311	D
12	E	62	B	112	C	162	C	212	D	262	A	312	B
13	E	63	C	113	B	163	C	213	E	263	D	313	E
14	B	64	C	114	A	164	C	214	E	264	B	314	A
15	C	65	A	115	B	165	G	215	F	265	A	315	D
16	B	66	C	116	A	166	D	216	D	266	B	316	C
17	B	67	D	117	A	167	D	217	D	267	A	317	E
18	C	68	C	118	D	168	C	218	D	268	B		
19	D	69	D	119	B	169	A	219	G	269	C		
20	C	70	A	120	C	170	D	220	D	270	E		
21	B	71	C	121	A	171	D	221	D	271	E		
22	A	72	B	122	D	172	D	222	B	272	A		
23	F	73	B	123	E	173	C	223	F	273	D		
24	D	74	A	124	B	174	B	224	D	274	B		
25	A	75	C	125	D	175	C	225	F	275	A		
26	B	76	B	126	A	176	E	226	E	276	B		
27	A	77	B	127	E	177	B	227	B	277	B		
28	F	78	A	128	C	178	E	228	F	278	B		
29	D	79	B	129	D	179	D	229	E	279	A		
30	A	80		130	C	180	B	230	C	280	D		
31	D	81	B	131	C	181	D	231	D	281	C		
32	D	82	A	132	C	182	D	232	D	282	B		
33	F	83	B	133	E	183	B	233	F	283	C		
34	B	84	E	134	B	184	C	234	D	284	B		
35	C	85	A	135	B	185	A	235	B	285	A		
36	B	86	C	136	A	186	A	236	D	286	C		
37	C	87	C	137	A	187	D	237	B	287	E		
38	A	88	B	138	B	188	C	238	A	288	C		

| 39 | A | 89 | C | 139 | B | 189 | B | 239 | C | 289 | C |
| 40 | C | 90 | C | 140 | A | 190 | C | 240 | C | 290 | E |

Q	A	Q	A	Q	A	Q	A	Q	A	Q	A
41	B	91	A	141	B	191	B	241	C	291	C
42	D	92	E	142	D	192	A	242	C	292	C
43	C	93	C	143	A	193	B	243	B	293	A
44	A	94	B	144	A	194	B	244	D	294	D
45	C	95	C	145	B	195	E	245	D	295	C
46	C	96	B	146	A	196	A	246	E	296	B
47	C	97	B	147	D	197	B	247	E	297	A
48	B	98	C	148	C	198	C	248	C	298	C
49	D	99	C	149	D	199	C	249	A	299	C
50	E	100	B	150	A	200	D	250	B	300	E

Worked Answers

Question 1: B

Each three-block combination is mutually exclusive to any other combination, so the probabilities are added. Each block pick is independent of all other picks, so the probabilities can be multiplied. For this scenario there are three possible combinations:

P(2 red blocks and 1 yellow block) = P(red then red then yellow) + P(red then yellow then red) + P(yellow then red then red) =

$$\left(\frac{12}{20} \times \frac{11}{19} \times \frac{8}{18}\right) + \left(\frac{12}{20} \times \frac{8}{19} \times \frac{11}{18}\right) + \left(\frac{8}{20} \times \frac{12}{19} \times \frac{11}{18}\right) =$$

$$\frac{3 \times 12 \times 11 \times 8}{20 \times 19 \times 18} = \frac{44}{95}$$

Question 2: C

Multiply through by 15: $3(3x + 5) + 5(2x - 2) = 18 \times 15$

Thus: $9x + 15 + 10x - 10 = 270$

$9x + 10x = 270 - 15 + 10$

$19x = 265$

$x = 13.95$

Question 3: C

This is a rare case where you need to factorise a complex polynomial:

(3x   )(x   ) = 0, possible pairs: 2 x 10, 10 x 2, 4 x 5, 5 x 4

(3x - 4)(x + 5) = 0

3x - 4 = 0, so x = $\frac{4}{3}$

x + 5 = 0, so x = -5

Question 4: C

$$\frac{5(x - 4)}{(x + 2)(x - 4)} + \frac{3(x + 2)}{(x + 2)(x - 4)}$$

$$= \frac{5x - 20 + 3x + 6}{(x + 2)(x - 4)}$$

$$= \frac{8x - 14}{(x + 2)(x - 4)}$$

Question 5: E

$p \propto \sqrt[3]{q}$, so $p = k\sqrt[3]{q}$

$p = 12$ when $q = 27$ gives $12 = k\sqrt[3]{27}$, so $12 = 3k$ and $k = 4$

so $p = 4\sqrt[3]{q}$

Now $p = 24$:

$24 = 4\sqrt[3]{q}$, so $6 = \sqrt[3]{q}$ and $q = 6^3 = 216$

Question 6: A

$8 \times 9 = 72$

$8 = (4 \times 2) = 2 \times 2 \times 2$

$9 = 3 \times 3$

$(2 \times 2 \times 2 \times 3 \times 3)^2 = 2 \times 2 \times 2 \times 2 \times 2 \times 2 \times 3 \times 3 \times 3 \times 3 = 2^6 \times 3^4$

Question 7: C

Note that $1.151 \times 2 = 2.302$.

Thus: $\dfrac{2 \times 10^5 + 2 \times 10^2}{10^{10}} = 2 \times 10^{-5} + 2 \times 10^{-8}$

$= 0.00002 + 0.00000002 = 0.00002002$

Question 8: E

$y^2 + ay + b$

$= (y + 2)^2 - 5 = y^2 + 4y + 4 - 5$

$= y^2 + 4y + 4 - 5 = y^2 + 4y - 1$

So $a = 4$ and $y = -1$

Question 9: E

Take $5(m + 4n)$ as a common factor to give: $\dfrac{4(m+4n)}{5(m+4n)} + \dfrac{5(m-2n)}{5(m+4n)}$

Simplify to give: $\dfrac{4m+16n+5m-10n}{5(m+4n)} = \dfrac{9m+6n}{5(m+4n)} = \dfrac{3(3m+2n)}{5(m+4n)}$

Question 10: C

$A \propto \dfrac{1}{\sqrt{B}}$. Thus, $= \dfrac{k}{\sqrt{B}}$.

Substitute the values in to give: $4 = \dfrac{k}{\sqrt{25}}$.

Thus, $k = 20$.

Therefore, $A = \frac{20}{\sqrt{B}}$.

When B = 16, $A = \frac{20}{\sqrt{16}} = \frac{20}{4} = 5$

Question 11: E

Angles SVU and STU are opposites and add up to 180°, so STU = 91°

The angle of the centre of a circle is twice the angle at the circumference so SOU = 2 x 91° = 182°

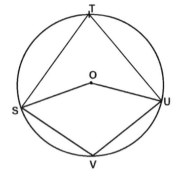

Question 12: E

The surface area of an open cylinder A = 2πrh. Cylinder B is an enlargement of A, so the increases in radius (r) and height (h) will be proportional: $\frac{r_A}{r_B} = \frac{h_A}{h_B}$. Let us call the proportion coefficient n, where $n = \frac{r_A}{r_B} = \frac{h_A}{h_B}$.

So $\frac{Area\ A}{Area\ B} = \frac{2\pi r_A h_A}{2\pi r_B h_B} = n\ x\ n = n^2$. $\frac{Area\ A}{Area\ B} = \frac{32\pi}{8\pi} = 4$, so n = 2.

The proportion coefficient n = 2 also applies to their volumes, where the third dimension (also radius, i.e. the r^2 in $V = \pi r^2 h$) is equally subject to this constant of proportionality. The cylinder's volumes are related by $n^3 = 8$.

If the smaller cylinder has volume 2π cm³, then the larger will have volume $2\pi\ x\ n^3 = 2\pi\ x\ 8 = 16\pi$ cm³.

Question 13: E

$= \frac{8}{x(3-x)} - \frac{6(3-x)}{x(3-x)}$

$= \frac{8 - 18 + 6x}{x(3-x)}$

$= \frac{6x - 10}{x(3-x)}$

Question 14: B

For the black ball to be drawn in the last round, white balls must be drawn every round. Thus the probability is given by $P = \frac{9}{10}\ x\ \frac{8}{9}\ x\ \frac{7}{8}\ x\ \frac{6}{7}\ x\ \frac{5}{6}\ x\ \frac{4}{5}\ x\ \frac{3}{4}\ x\ \frac{2}{3}\ x\ \frac{1}{2}$

$= \frac{9\ x\ 8\ x\ 7\ x\ 6\ x\ 5\ x\ 4\ x\ 3\ x\ 2\ x\ 1}{10\ x\ 9\ x\ 8\ x\ 7\ x\ 6\ x\ 5\ x\ 4\ x\ 3\ x\ 2\ x\ 1} = \frac{1}{10}$

Question 15: C

The probability of getting a king the first time is $\frac{4}{52} = \frac{1}{13}$, and the probability of getting a king the second time is $\frac{3}{51}$. These are independent events, thus, the probability of drawing two kings is $\frac{1}{13}\ x\ \frac{3}{51} = \frac{3}{663} = \frac{1}{221}$

Question 16: B

The probabilities of all outcomes must sum to one, so if the probability of rolling a 1 is x, then: $x + x + x + x + 2x = 1$. Therefore, $x = \frac{1}{7}$.

The probability of obtaining two sixes $P_{12} = \frac{2}{7} \times \frac{2}{7} = \frac{4}{49}$

Question 17: B

There are plenty of ways of counting, however the easiest is as follows: 0 is divisible by both 2 and 3. Half of the numbers from 1 to 36 are even (i.e. 18 of them). 3, 9, 15, 21, 27, 33 are the only numbers divisible by 3 that we've missed. There are 25 outcomes divisible by 2 or 3, out of 37.

Question 18: C

List the six ways of achieving this outcome: HHTT, HTHT, HTTH, TTHH, THTH and THHT. There are 2^4 possible outcomes for 4 consecutive coin flips, so the probability of two heads and two tails is: $6 \times \frac{1}{2^4} = \frac{6}{16} = \frac{3}{8}$

Question 19: D

Count the number of ways to get a 5, 6 or 7 (draw the square if helpful). The ways to get a 5 are: 1, 4; 2, 3; 3, 2; 4, 1. The ways to get a 6 are: 1, 5; 2, 4; 3, 3; 4, 2; 5, 1. The ways to get a 7 are: 1, 6; 2, 5; 3, 4; 4, 3; 5, 2; 6, 1. That is 15 out of 36 possible outcomes.

	1	2	3	4	5	6
1	2	3	4	5	6	7
2	3	4	5	6	7	8
3	4	5	6	7	8	9
4	5	6	7	8	9	10
5	6	7	8	9	10	11
6	7	8	9	10	11	12

Question 20: C

There are x+y+z balls in the bag, and the probability of picking a red ball is $\frac{x}{(x+y+z)}$ and the probability of picking a green ball is $\frac{z}{(x+y+z)}$. These are independent events, so the probability of picking red then green is $\frac{xz}{(x+y+z)^2}$ and the probability of picking green then red is the same. These outcomes are mutually exclusive, so are added.

Question 21: B

There are two ways of doing it, pulling out a red ball then a blue ball, or pulling out a blue ball and then a red ball. Let us work out the probability of the first: $\frac{x}{(x+y+z)} \times \frac{y}{x+y+z-1}$, and the probability of the second option will be the same. These are mutually exclusive options, so the probabilities may be summed.

Question 22: A

[x: Player 1 wins point, y: Player 2 wins point]

Player 1 wins in five rounds if we get: yxxxx, xyxxx, xxyxx, xxxyx.

(Note the case of xxxxy would lead to player 1 winning in 4 rounds, which the question forbids.)

Each of these have a probability of $p^4(1-p)$. Thus, the solution is $4p^4(1-p)$.

Question 23: F

$4x + 7 + 18x + 20 = 14$

$22x + 27 = 14$

Thus, $22x = -13$

Giving $x = -\frac{13}{22}$

Question 24: D

$r^3 = \dfrac{3V}{4\pi}$

Thus, $r = \left(\dfrac{3V}{4\pi}\right)^{1/3}$

Therefore, $S = 4\pi \left[\left(\dfrac{3V}{4\pi}\right)^{\frac{1}{3}}\right]^2 = 4\pi \left(\dfrac{3V}{4\pi}\right)^{\frac{2}{3}}$

$= \dfrac{4\pi(3V)^{\frac{2}{3}}}{(4\pi)^{\frac{2}{3}}} = (3V)^{\frac{2}{3}} \times \dfrac{(4\pi)^1}{(4\pi)^{\frac{2}{3}}}$

$= (3V)^{\frac{2}{3}}(4\pi)^{1-\frac{2}{3}} = (4\pi)^{\frac{1}{3}}(3V)^{\frac{2}{3}}$

Question 25: A

Let each unit length be x.

Thus, $S = 6x^2$. Therefore, $x = \left(\dfrac{S}{6}\right)^{\frac{1}{2}}$

$V = x^3$. Thus, $V = [\left(\dfrac{S}{6}\right)^{\frac{1}{2}}]^3$ so $V = \left(\dfrac{S}{6}\right)^{\frac{3}{2}}$

Question 26: B

Multiplying the second equation by 2 we get 4x + 16y = 24. Subtracting the first equation from this we get 13y = 17, so $y = \frac{17}{13}$. Then solving for x we get $x = \frac{10}{13}$. You could also try substituting possible solutions one by one, although given that the equations are both linear and contain easy numbers, it is quicker to solve them algebraically.

Question 27: A

Multiply by the denominator to give: $(7x + 10) = (3y^2 + 2)(9x + 5)$

Partially expand brackets on right side: $(7x + 10) = 9x(3y^2 + 2) + 5(3y^2 + 2)$

Take x terms across to left side: $7x - 9x(3y^2 + 2) = 5(3y^2 + 2) - 10$

Take x outside the brackets: $x[7 - 9(3y^2 + 2)] = 5(3y^2 + 2) - 10$

Thus: $x = \frac{5(3y^2 + 2) - 10}{7 - 9(3y^2 + 2)}$

Simplify to give: $x = \frac{(15y^2)}{(7 - 9(3y^2 + 2))}$

Question 28: F

$$3x\left(\frac{3x^7}{x^{\frac{1}{3}}}\right)^3 = 3x\left(\frac{3^3 x^{21}}{x^{\frac{3}{3}}}\right)$$

$$= 3x\,\frac{27x^{21}}{x} = 81x^{21}$$

Question 29: D

$$2x[2^{\frac{7}{14}}\,x^{\frac{7}{14}}] = 2x[2^{\frac{1}{2}}\,x^{\frac{1}{2}}]$$

$$= 2x(\sqrt{2}\,\sqrt{x}) = 2\left[\sqrt{x}\sqrt{x}\right][\sqrt{2}\,\sqrt{x}]$$

$$= 2\sqrt{2x^3}$$

Question 30: A

$A = \pi r^2$, therefore $10\pi = \pi r^2$

Thus, $r = \sqrt{10}$

Therefore, the circumference is $2\pi\sqrt{10}$

Question 31: D

$3.4 = 12 + (3 + 4) = 19$

$19.5 = 95 + (19 + 5) = 119$

Question 32: D

$2.3 = \dfrac{2^3}{2} = 4$

$4.2 = \dfrac{4^2}{4} = 4$

Question 33: F

This is a tricky question that requires you to know how to 'complete the square':

$(x + 1.5)(x + 1.5) = x^2 + 3x + 2.25$

Thus, $(x + 1.5)^2 - 7.25 = x^2 + 3x - 5 = 0$

Therefore, $(x + 1.5)^2 = 7.25 = \dfrac{29}{4}$

Thus, $x + 1.5 = \sqrt{\frac{29}{4}}$

Thus $x = -\frac{3}{2} \pm \sqrt{\frac{29}{4}} = -\frac{3}{2} \pm \frac{\sqrt{29}}{2}$

Question 34: B

Whilst you definitely need to solve this graphically, it is necessary to complete the square for the first equation to allow you to draw it more easily:

$(x + 2)^2 = x^2 + 4x + 4$

Thus, $y = (x + 2)^2 + 10 = x^2 + 4x + 14$

This is now an easy curve to draw ($y = x^2$ that has moved 2 units left and 10 units up). The turning point of this quadratic is to the left and well above anything in x^3, so the only solution is the first intersection of the two curves in the upper right quadrant around (3.4, 39).

Question 35: C

The easiest way to solve this is to sketch them (don't waste time solving them algebraically). As soon as you've done this, it'll be very obvious that y = 2 and $y = 1-x^2$ don't intersect, since the latter has its turning point at (0, 1) and zero points at x = -1 and 1. y = x and $y = x^2$ intersect at the origin and (1, 1), and y = 2 runs through both.

Question 36: B

Notice that you're not required to get the actual values – just the number's magnitude. Thus, 897653 can be approximated to 900,000 and 0.009764 to 0.01. Therefore, 900,000 x 0.01 = 9,000

Question 37: C

Multiply through by 70: $7(7x + 3) + 10(3x + 1) = 14 \times 70$

Simplify: $49x + 21 + 30x + 10 = 980$

$79x + 31 = 980$

$x = \frac{949}{79}$

Question 38: A

Split the equilateral triangle into 2 right-angled triangles and apply Pythagoras' theorem:

$x^2 = \left(\frac{x}{2}\right)^2 + h^2$. Thus $h^2 = \frac{3}{4}x^2$

$h = \sqrt{\frac{3x^2}{4}} = \frac{\sqrt{3x^2}}{2}$

The area of a triangle = ½ x base x height $= \frac{1}{2} x \frac{\sqrt{3x^2}}{2}$

Simplifying gives: $x \frac{\sqrt{3x^2}}{4} = x \frac{\sqrt{3}\sqrt{x^2}}{4} = \frac{x^2\sqrt{3}}{4}$

Question 39: A

This is a question testing your ability to spot 'the difference between two squares'.

Factorise to give: $3 - \dfrac{7x(5x-1)(5x+1)}{(7x)^2(5x+1)}$

Cancel out: $3 - \dfrac{(5x-1)}{7x}$

Question 40: C

The easiest way to do this is to 'complete the square':

$(x-5)^2 = x^2 - 10x + 25$

Thus, $(x-5)^2 - 125 = x^2 - 10x - 100 = 0$

Therefore, $(x-5)^2 = 125$

$x - 5 = \pm\sqrt{125} = \pm\sqrt{25}\,\sqrt{5} = \pm 5\sqrt{5}$

$x = 5 \pm 5\sqrt{5}$

Question 41: B

Factorise by completing the square:

$x^2 - 4x + 7 = (x-2)^2 + 3$

Simplify: $(x-2)^2 = y^3 + 2 - 3$

$x - 2 = \pm\sqrt{y^3 - 1}$

$x = 2 \pm \sqrt{y^3 - 1}$

Question 42: D

Square both sides to give: $(3x+2)^2 = 7x^2 + 2x + y$

Thus: $y = (3x+2)^2 - 7x^2 - 2x = (9x^2 + 12x + 4) - 7x^2 - 2x$

$y = 2x^2 + 10x + 4$

Question 43: C

This is a fourth order polynomial, which you aren't expected to be able to factorise at GCSE. This is where looking at the options makes your life a lot easier. In all of them, opening the bracket on the right side involves making $(y \pm 1)^4$ on the left side, i.e. the answers are hinting that $(y \pm 1)^4$ is the solution to the fourth order polynomial.

Since there are negative terms in the equations (e.g. $-4y^3$), the solution has to be:

$(y-1)^4 = y^4 - 4y^3 + 6y^2 - 4y + 1$

Therefore, $(y-1)^4 + 1 = x^5 + 7$

Thus, $y - 1 = (x^5 + 6)^{\frac{1}{4}}$

$y = 1 + (x^5 + 6)^{1/4}$

Question 44: A

Let the width of the television be 4x and the height of the television be 3x.

Then by Pythagoras: $(4x)^2 + (3x)^2 = 50^2$

Simplify: $25x^2 = 2500$

Thus: $x = 10$. Therefore: the screen is 30 inches by 40 inches, i.e. the area is 1,200 inches².

Question 45: C

Square both sides to give: $1 + \frac{3}{x^2} = (y^5 + 1)^2$

Multiply out: $\frac{3}{x^2} = (y^{10} + 2y^5 + 1) - 1$

Thus: $x^2 = \frac{3}{y^{10}+2y^5}$

Therefore: $x = \sqrt{\frac{3}{y^{10} + 2y^5}}$

Question 46: C

The easiest way is to double the first equation and triple the second to get:

$6x - 10y = 20 \; and \; 6x + 6y = 39.$

Subtract the first from the second to give: $16y = 19,$

Therefore, $y = \frac{19}{16}.$

Substitute back into the first equation to give $x = \frac{85}{16}.$

Question 47: C

This is fairly straightforward; the first inequality is the easier one to work with: B and D and E violate it, so we just need to check A and C in the second inequality.

C: $1^3 - 2^2 < 3$, but A: $2^3 - 1^2 > 3$

Question 48: B

Whilst this can be done graphically, it's quicker to do algebraically (because the second equation is not as easy to sketch). Intersections occur where the curves have the same coordinates.

Thus: $x + 4 = 4x^2 + 5x + 5$

Simplify: $4x^2 + 4x + 1 = 0$

Factorise: $(2x + 1)(2x + 1) = 0$

Thus, the two graphs only intersect once at $x = -\frac{1}{2}$

Question 49: D

It's better to do this algebraically as the equations are easy to work with and you would need to sketch very accurately to get the answer. Intersections occur where the curves have the same coordinates. Thus: $x^3 = x$

$x^3 - x = 0$

Thus: $x(x^2 - 1) = 0$

Spot the 'difference between two squares': $x(x + 1)(x - 1) = 0$

Thus there are 3 intersections: at $x = 0, 1 \text{ and} - 1$

Question 50: E

Note that the line is the hypotenuse of a right angled triangle with one side unit length and one side of length ½. By Pythagoras, $\left(\frac{1}{2}\right)^2 + 1^2 = x^2$

Thus, $x^2 = \frac{1}{4} + 1 = \frac{5}{4}$

$x = \sqrt{\frac{5}{4}} = \frac{\sqrt{5}}{\sqrt{4}} = \frac{\sqrt{5}}{2}$

Question 51: D

We can eliminate z from equation (1) and (2) by multiplying equation (1) by 3 and adding it to equation (2):

3x + 3y – 3z = -3	Equation (1) multiplied by 3
2x – 2y +3z = 8	Equation (2) then add both equations
5x + y = 5	We label this as equation (4)

Now we must eliminate the same variable z from another pair of equations by using equation (1) and (3):

2x + 2y – 2z = -2	Equation (1) multiplied by 2
2x – y + 2z = 9	Equation (3) then add both equations
4x + y = 7	We label this as equation (5)

We now use both equations (4) and (5) to obtain the value of x:

5x + y = 5	Equation (4)
- 4x - y = -7	Equation (5) multiplied by -1
x = -2	

Substitute x back in to calculate y:

$4x + y = 7$

$4(-2) + y = 7$

$- 8 + y = 7$

$y = 15$

Substitute x and y back in to calculate z:

$x + y - z = -1$

$-2 + 15 - z = -1$

$13 - z = -1$

$-z = -14$

$z = 14$

Thus: $x = -2, y = 15, z = 14$

Question 52: D

This is one of the easier maths questions. Take $3a$ as a factor to give:

$$3a(a^2 - 10a + 25) = 3a(a - 5)\,(a - 5) = 3a(a - 5)^2$$

Question 53: B

Note that 12 is the Lowest Common Multiple of 3 and 4. Thus:

$-3 (4x + 3y) = -3 (48)$ Multiply each side by -3

$4 (3x + 2y) = 4 (34)$ Multiply each side by 4

$-12x - 9y = -144$

$\underline{12x + 8y = 136}$ Add together

$-y = -8$

$y = 8$

Substitute y back in:

$4x + 3y = 48$

$4x + 3(8) = 48$

$4x + 24 = 48$

$4x = 24$

$x = 6$

Question 54: E

Don't be fooled, this is an easy question, just obey BODMAS and don't skip steps.

$\frac{-(25-28)^2}{-36+14} = \frac{-(-3)^2}{-22}$

This gives: $\frac{-(9)}{-22} = \frac{9}{22}$

Question 55: E

Since there are 26 possible letters for each of the 3 letters in the license plate, and there are 10 possible numbers (0-9) for each of the 3 numbers in the same plate, then the number of license plates would be:

$(26) \times (26) \times (26) \times (10) \times (10) \times (10) = 17,576,000$

Question 56: B

Expand the brackets to give: $4x^2 - 12x + 9 = 0$.

Factorise: $(2x - 3)(2x - 3) = 0$.

Thus, only one solution exists, x = 1.5.

Note that you could also use the fact that the discriminant, $b^2 - 4ac = 0$ to get the answer.

Question 57: C

$= \left(x^{\frac{1}{2}}\right)^{\frac{1}{2}} (y^{-3})^{\frac{1}{2}}$

$= x^{\frac{1}{4}} y^{-\frac{3}{2}} = \frac{x^{\frac{1}{4}}}{y^{\frac{3}{2}}}$

Question 58: A

Let x, y, and z represent the rent for the 1-bedroom, 2-bedroom, and 3-bedroom flats, respectively. We can write 3 different equations: 1 for the rent, 1 for the repairs, and the last one for the statement that the 3-bedroom unit costs twice as much as the 1-bedroom unit.

(1) x + y + z = 1240

(2) 0.1x + 0.2y + 0.3z = 276

(3) z = 2x

Substitute z = 2x in both of the two other equations to eliminate z:

(4) x + y + 2x = 3x + y = 1240

(5) 0.1x + 0.2y + 0.3(2x) = 0.7x + 0.2y = 276

-2(3x + y) = -2(1240)   Multiply each side of (4) by -2

10(0.7x + 0.2y) = 10(276)   Multiply each side of (5) by 10

(6) -6x -2y = -2480   Add these 2 equations

(7) 7x + 2y = 2760

x = 280

z = 2(280) = 560   Because z = 2x

280 + y + 560 = 1240   Because x + y + z = 1240

y = 400

Thus the units rent for £ 280, £ 400, £ 560 per week respectively.

Question 59: C

Following BODMAS:

$$= 5 \left[5(6^2 - 5 \times 3) + 400^{\frac{1}{2}}\right]^{1/3} + 7$$

$$= 5 \left[5(36 - 15) + 20\right]^{\frac{1}{3}} + 7$$

$$= 5 \left[5(21) + 20\right]^{\frac{1}{3}} + 7$$

$$= 5 \left(105 + 20\right)^{\frac{1}{3}} + 7$$

$$= 5 \left(125\right)^{\frac{1}{3}} + 7$$

$$= 5 (5) + 7$$

$$= 25 + 7 = 32$$

Question 60: B

Consider a triangle formed by joining the centre to two adjacent vertices. Six triangles can be made around the centre – thus, the central angle is 60 degrees. the two lines forming the triangle are of equal length, we have 6 identical equilateral triangles in the hexagon.

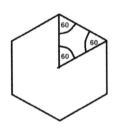

similar

Since

Now split the triangle in half and apply Pythagoras' theorem:

$$1^2 = 0.5^2 + h^2$$

Thus, $h = \sqrt{\frac{3}{4}} = \frac{\sqrt{3}}{2}$

Thus, the area of the triangle is: $\frac{1}{2}bh = \frac{1}{2} \times 1 \times \frac{\sqrt{3}}{2} = \frac{\sqrt{3}}{4}$

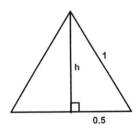

Therefore, the area of the hexagon is: $\frac{\sqrt{3}}{4} \times 6 = \frac{3\sqrt{3}}{2}$

Question 61: B

Let x be the width and x+19 be the length.

Thus, the area of a rectangle is $x(x + 19) = 780$.

Therefore:

$x^2 + 19x - 780 = 0$

$(x - 20)(x + 39) = 0$

$x - 20 = 0$ or $x + 39 = 0$

$x = 20$ or $x = -39$

Since length can never be a negative number, we disregard $x = -39$ and use $x = 20$ instead.

Thus, the width is 20 metres and the length is 39 metres.

Question 62: B

The quickest way to solve is by trial and error, substituting the provided options. However, if you're keen to do this algebraically, you can do the following:

Start by setting up the equations: Perimeter = $2L + 2W = 34$

Thus: $L + W = 17$

Using Pythagoras: $L^2 + W^2 = 13^2$

Since $L + W = 17$, $W = 17 - L$

Therefore: $L^2 + (17 - L)^2 = 169$

$L^2 + 289 - 34L + L^2 = 169$

$2L^2 - 34L + 120 = 0$

$L^2 - 17L + 60 = 0$

$(L - 5)(L - 12) = 0$

Thus: $L = 5$ and $L = 12$

And: $W = 12$ and $W = 5$

Question 63: C

Multiply both sides by 8: $4(3x - 5) + 2(x + 5) = 8(x + 1)$

Remove brackets: $12x - 20 + 2x + 10 = 8x + 8$

Simplify: $14x - 10 = 8x + 8$

Add 10: $14x = 8x + 18$

Subtract 8x: $6x = 18$

Therefore: $x = 3$

Question 64: C

Recognise that 1.742 x 3 is 5.226. Now, the original equation simplifies to: $= \frac{3 \times 10^6 + 3 \times 10^5}{10^{10}}$

$= 3 \times 10^{-4} + 3 \times 10^{-5} = 3.3 \times 10^{-4}$

Question 65: A

$Area = \frac{(2+\sqrt{2})(4-\sqrt{2})}{2}$

$= \frac{8 - 2\sqrt{2} + 4\sqrt{2} - 2}{2}$

$= \frac{6 + 2\sqrt{2}}{2}$

$= 3 + \sqrt{2}$

Question 66: C

Square both sides: $\frac{4}{x} + 9 = (y-2)^2$

$\frac{4}{x} = (y-2)^2 - 9$

Cross Multiply: $\frac{x}{4} = \frac{1}{(y-2)^2 - 9}$

$x = \frac{4}{y^2 - 4y + 4 - 9}$

Factorise: $x = \frac{4}{y^2 - 4y - 5}$

$x = \frac{4}{(y+1)(y-5)}$

Question 67: D

Set up the equation: $5x - 5 = 0.5(6x + 2)$

$10x - 10 = 6x + 2$

$4x = 12$

$x = 3$

Question 68: C

Round numbers appropriately: $\frac{55 + (\frac{9}{4})^2}{\sqrt{900}} = \frac{55 + \frac{81}{16}}{30}$

81 rounds to 80 to give: $\frac{55 + 5}{30} = \frac{60}{30} = 2$

Question 69: D

There are three outcomes from choosing the type of cheese in the crust. For each of the additional toppings to possibly add, there are 2 outcomes: 1 to include and another not to include a certain topping, for each of the 7 toppings

Thus, the number of different kinds of pizza is: 3 x 2 x 2 x 2 x 2 x 2 x 2 x 2 = 3 x 2^7

= 3 x 128 = 384

Question 70: A

Although it is possible to do this algebraically, by far the easiest way is via trial and error. The clue that you shouldn't attempt it algebraically is the fact that rearranging the first equation to make x or y the subject leaves you with a difficult equation to work with (e.g. $x = \sqrt{1 - y^2}$) when you try to substitute in the second.

An exceptionally good student might notice that the equations are symmetric in x and y, i.e. the solution is when x = y. Thus $2x^2 = 1$ and $2x = \sqrt{2}$ which gives $\frac{\sqrt{2}}{2}$ as the answer.

Question 71: C

$f(x) = 0 \implies 16x^4 + 32x^3 + 24x^2 + 8x + 1$

$(2x + 1)^4 = x^4$

This means that $2x + 1 = \pm x \implies x = -\frac{1}{3}$ or -1

Question 72: B

Rearrange the equation: $x^2 + x - 6 \geq 0$

Factorise: $(x + 3)(x - 2) \geq 0$

Remember that this is a quadratic inequality so requires a quick sketch to ensure you don't make a silly mistake with which way the sign is.

Thus, $y = 0$ when $x = 2$ and $x = -3$. $y > 0$ when $x > 2$ or $x < -3$.

Thus, the solution is: $x \leq -3 \ and \ x \geq 2$.

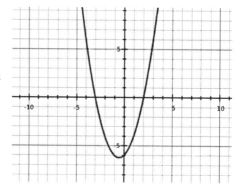

Question 73: B

Using Pythagoras: $a^2 + b^2 = x^2$

Since the triangle is equilateral: $a = b, \ so \ 2a^2 = x^2$

Area $= \frac{1}{2} base \ x \ height = \frac{1}{2}a^2$. From above, $a^2 = \frac{x^2}{2}$

Thus, the area $= \frac{1}{2} x \frac{x^2}{2} = \frac{x^2}{4}$

Question 74: A

If X and Y are doubled, the value of Q increases by 4. Halving the value of A reduces this to 2. Finally, tripling the value of B reduces this to ⅔, i.e. the value decreases by ⅓.

Question 75: C

The quickest way to do this is to sketch the curves. This requires you to factorise both equations by completing the square:

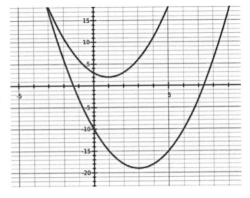

$$x^2 - 2x + 3 = (x-1)^2 + 2$$

$x^2 - 6x - 10 = (x-3)^2 - 19$ Thus, the first equation has a turning point at $(1, 2)$ and doesn't cross the x-axis. The second equation has a turning point at $(3, -19)$ and crosses the x-axis twice.

Question 76: B

Let tail = T, body and legs = B and head = H.

As described in the question H = T + 0.5B and B = T + H.

We have already been told that T = 30Kg.

Therefore, substitute the second equation into the first as H = 30 + 0.5(30 + H).

Re-arranging reveals that -0.5H = 45Kg and therefore the weight of the head is 90Kg, the body and legs 120Kg and as we were told the tail weighs 30Kg.

Thus, giving a total weight of 240Kg

Question 77: B

Expand the larger scientific number so that it reads 10 to the power 6 like so: $4.2 \times 10^{10} = 42000 \times 10^6$. Now that the powers are the same across the numerators, a simple subtraction can be performed $(42000 - 4.2) \times 10^6 = 41995.8 \times 10^6$ which can be simplified to 4.19958×10^{10}. Next consider the division which can be competed in a two-step process, first divide the numerator by 2 like so $(4.19958/2) \times 10^{10} = 2.09979 \times 10^{10}$ and then subtract the powers like so $2.09979 \times 10^{(10-3)} = 2.09979 \times 10^7$.

Question 78: A

Note the triangle formed by the right-angle lines and the tangent. Recall that as this is a right-angle triangle then the other two angles must be 45°. As angles along a straight line add up to 180°, a must equal $180 - 45 = 135^0$. Angles around the origin must add up to 360o and therefore $b = (360 - 90)/2 = 135^0$. Therefore, the correct answer is A.

Question 79: B

The probability of drawing a blue ball (1/21) and then a black ball (1/20) is $1/21 \times 1/20 = 1/420$. However, note that it is also possible that these balls could also be drawn out in the opposite order. Therefore, the probability must be multiplied by two like so $1/420 \times 2 = 2/420 = 1/210$.

Question 80: D

To answer this, you need to change one equivalent function to another:

$$y = 9x^{-\frac{1}{3}} = \frac{9}{x^{\frac{1}{3}}} = \frac{9}{\sqrt[3]{x}}$$

Question 81: B

Start by multiplying each term by ax to give: $a(y+x)=x^2+a^2$

Expand the brackets: $ay + ax = x^2 + a^2$

Subtract ax from both sides: $ay = x^2 + a^2 - ax$

Lastly, divide the both sides by a to get: $y = \frac{x^2+a^2-ax}{a}$

Question 82: A

The equation for a circle, with centre at the origin and radius r is $x^2 + y^2 = r^2$

The equation of this circle is therefore $x^2 + y^2 = 25$

Solve the problem using simultaneous equations or by drawing the line onto the graph.

$x^2 + (3x - 5)^2 = 25$

This simplifies to $10x^2 - 30x = 0$

$10x(x - 3) = 0$

So $x = 3$ or $x = 0$ where the two graphs intersect

Question 83: C

Number of annual flights = Flights per hour × Number of hours in one year × Number of airports

$= 4 \times (24 \times 365) \times 1000$

$= 96 \times 365 \times (1000)$

$\approx 100 \times 365 \times 10 \times 100$

$= 365 \times 10^5 = 36.5 \text{ Million}$

Question 84: E

The way to solve this is to break the calculation down into parts, almost working backwards. The number of seconds in 66 weeks is given by:

$= 60 \times 60 \times 24 \times 7 \times 66:$

$= (10 \times 6) \times (12 \times 5) \times (4 \times 6) \times 7 \times (11 \times 6)$

$= 1 \times 4 \times 5 \times 6 \times 6 \times 6 \times 7 \times 10 \times 11 \times 12$

$= 1 \times 4 \times 5 \times 6 \times (6) \times 7 \times 10 \times 11 \times (12 \times 6)$

$= 1 \times 4 \times 5 \times 6 \times (3 \times 2) \times 7 \times 10 \times 11 \times (72)$

$= 1 \times 2 \times 3 \times 4 \times 5 \times 6 \times 7 \times 10 \times 11 \times (9 \times 8)$

$= 1 \times 2 \times 3 \times 4 \times 5 \times 6 \times 7 \times 8 \times 9 \times 10 \times 11 = 11!$

Question 85: A

Write $\frac{\sqrt{20}-2}{\sqrt{5}+3}$ in the form $p\sqrt{5} + q$

Firstly, multiply the term by $\frac{\sqrt{5}-3}{\sqrt{5}-3}$ (i.e. 1) and write $\sqrt{20}$ as $2\sqrt{5}$

This gives: $\frac{10-6\sqrt{5}-2\sqrt{5}+6}{5-9}$

This simplifies to: $\frac{16-8\sqrt{5}}{-4}$

This simplifies to: $2\sqrt{5} - 4$

Therefore $p = 2$ and $q = -4$

Question 86: C

ABC and DBE are similar triangles because all of the angles are equal.

Therefore:

$\frac{BE}{BC} = \frac{DE}{AC}$

This is the case because the side lengths of the small and large triangles are in proportion to each other. Substitute the side lengths into the expression:

$\frac{4}{6} = \frac{DE}{9}$

DE = 6cm

Question 87: C

The formula for calculating compound interest can be given as investment x (interest rate^{years}) or in shorthand for this situation: $1687.5 = 500x^3$. Therefore, in order to calculate the interest rate the above formula must be rearranged to $\sqrt[3]{1687.5/500} = 1.5$ revealing an interest rate of 50%.

Question 88: B

To win one game, Rupert must win one squash game and one tennis game. In order to calculate the probability one winning one game, it is necessary to add the probability of winning one tennis game and losing one squash game to the probability of losing one tennis game and winning one squash game. The following calculation must be performed: $(\frac{3}{4} \times \frac{2}{3}) + (\frac{1}{4} \times \frac{1}{3}) = \frac{7}{12}$

Question 89: C

The formula for the sum of internal angles in a regular polygon is given by: $180(n - 2)$, where n is the number of sides of the polygon.

Thus: $180(n - 2) = 150 \times n$
$180n - 360 = 150n$
$3n = 36$

$n = 12$

Each side is 15cm so the perimeter is 12 x 15cm = 180cm.

Question 90: C

Let $y = 1.25$ x 10^8; this is not necessary, but helpful, as the question can then be expressed as: $\frac{100y + 10y}{2y} = \frac{110y}{2y} = 55$

Question 91: A

Equate y to give:

$2x - 1 = x^2 - 1$

$\rightarrow x^2 - 2x = 0$

$\rightarrow x(x - 2) = 0$

Thus, $x = 2$ and $x = 0$

There is no need to substitute back to get the y values as only option A satisfies the x values.

Question 92: E

Firstly, deal with the term in the brackets: $3^3=27$

$(x^{\frac{1}{2}})^3 = x^{1.5}$

$(3x^{\frac{1}{2}})^3 = 27x^{1.5}$

Next, divide by $3x^2$: $\frac{27}{3} = 9$

$\frac{x^{1.5}}{x^2} = x^{-0.5} = \frac{1}{\sqrt{x}}$

Answer $= \frac{9}{\sqrt{x}}$

Question 93: C

Remember the interior angles of a pentagon add up to 540° (three internal triangles), so each interior angle is 540/5 = 108°. Therefore, angle **a** is 108°. Recalling that angles within a quadrilateral sum to 360°, we can calculate **b**. The larger angle in the central quadrilateral is 360° – 2 x 108° (angles at a point) = 144°. Therefore, the remaining angle, **b** = (360 – 2(144)]/2 = 36°. The product of 36 and 108 is 3,888°.

Question 94: B

The ruler and the cruise ship look to be the same size because their edges are in line with Tim's line of sight. His eyes form the apex of two similar triangles. All the sides of two similar triangles are in the same ratio since the angles are the same, therefore:

$$\frac{0.3m}{X\,m} = \frac{1\,m}{1\,m + 999\,m}$$

Thus, $X\,m = 1000\,m \times \frac{0.3\,m}{1\,m}$

$1000 \times 0.3 = 300\,m$

Question 95: C

Let Bob = B, Kerry = K and Son = S.

$B = 2K, K = 3S$ and $B + K + S = 50$

$$50 = 2K + K + \frac{K}{3} = \frac{6K}{3} + \frac{3K}{3} + \frac{K}{3}$$

$$50 = \frac{10K}{3}$$

Hence: $10K = 150$

$K = 15$

$B = 2 \times 15 = 30$

$S = \frac{15}{3} = 5$

So: Bob's age when his son was born = 30 – 5 = 25.

Question 96: B

The mean is the sum of all the numbers in the set divided by the number of members in the set. The sum of all the numbers in the original set must be: 11 numbers × mean of 6 = 66. The sum of all the numbers once two are removed must then be: 9 numbers x mean of 5 = 45. Thus, any two numbers which sum to 66 – 45 = 21 could have been removed from the set. 6 and 9 are the only two number option available which does not sum to 21.

Question 97: B

Let $y = 3.4 \times 10^{10}$; this is not necessary, but helpful, as the question can then be expressed as:

$$\frac{10y + y}{200y} = \frac{11y}{200y} = \frac{11}{200} = \frac{5.5}{100}$$

$$= 5.5 \times 10^{-2}$$

Question 98: C

The radius and tangent to a circle always form a right angle, so using Pythagoras:

$3^2 + 4^2 = X^2$

$X = 5$ m

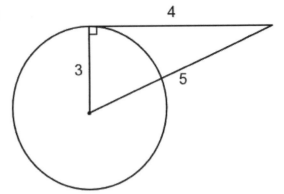

Question 99: C

Solve as simultaneous equations

Start by substituting $x = \frac{y}{3}$ into equation B.

This gives $y = \frac{18}{y} - 7$

Multiply every term by y to give:

$0 = y^2 + 7y - 18$

Factorise this quadratic to give:

$0 = (y + 9)(y - 2)$

Where the graphs meet, y is equal to 2 and 9. Then $y = 3x$ so the graphs meet when $x = 6$ and $x = 27$

Question 100: B

Equate the volume with the surface area in the proportion instructed by the question. $3(\frac{4}{3}\pi r^3) = 4\pi r^2$, simplifies to $r = 1$.

Question 101: B

The shortest distance between points A and B is a direct line. Using Pythagoras:

The diagonal of a sports field $= \sqrt{40^2 + 30^2} = \sqrt{1,600 + 900} = \sqrt{2,500} = 50$.

The diagonal between the sports fields $= \sqrt{4^2 + 3^2} = \sqrt{16 + 9} = \sqrt{25} = 5$.

Thus, the shortest distance between A and B $= 50 + 5 + 50 = 105\ m$.

Question 102: F

$1 + (3\sqrt{2} - 1)^2 + (3 + \sqrt{2})^2$

$= 1 + (18 - 2(3\sqrt{2}) + 1) + (9 + 2(3\sqrt{2}) + 2)$

$= 31 - 6\sqrt{2} + 6\sqrt{2} = \underline{31}$

Question 103: D

It is extremely helpful to draw diagrams to simplify this.

Shaded area = area of circle – area of square

The area of the circle is $\pi r^2 = 3 \times 12 = 3cm^2$.

We don't know the side length of the square, but we do know the 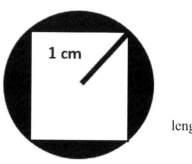 length of the diagonal is 2 cm, splitting the shape into two triangles.

The hypotenuse is therefore = $radius \times 2 = 2$

Using Pythagoras' theorem, $2^2 = x^2 + x^2$ (where x = length and width of square)

Hence $2x^2 = 4$

$x^2 = 2 =$ the area of the square

Therefore, the shaded area $= 3 - 2 = 1cm^2$

Question 104: D

The first step is to multiply out $(3p + 5)^2$

$(3p + 5)(3p + 5) = 24p + 49$

$9p^2 + 30p + 25 = 24p + 49$

$9p^2 + 6p - 24 = 0$

Then put the quadratic into brackets.

$\times \quad (3p + 6)(3p - 4) = 0$

Therefore, p must equal -6 or $+4$.

Question 105: E

From the rules of angles made by intersections with parallel lines, all of the angles marked with the same letter are equal. There is no way to find if d = 90°, only that b + d = c = 180° – a = 135°, so b is unknown.

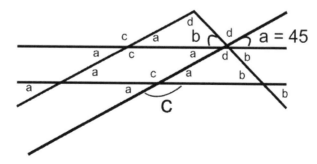

Question 106: B

We know that the product of slopes of perpendicular lines equals -1. Therefore:

$(n + 1)(n + 3) = -1$.

$n^2 + 4n + 3 = -1$

$n^2 + 4n + 4 = 0$

Factorising gives $(n + 2)(n + 2)$, therefore $n = -2$ for the lines to be perpendicular.

Question 107: C

The numerator of the fraction consists of 3 distinct terms or 3 distinct dimensions. As all other functions within the equation are constants one would consider this the volume of a complex 3D shape.

Question 108: E

Begin by drawing your line of best fit, remembering not to force it through the origin. Begin fitting the general equation y = mx + c to your line. Calculate the gradient as Δy/Δx and read the y intercept off your annotated graph.

Question 109: C

Solve as simultaneous equations

Start by substituting $x = \frac{y}{3}$ into equation B.

This gives $y = \frac{18}{y} - 7$

Multiply every term by y to give:

$0 = y2 + 7y - 18$

Factorise this quadratic to give:

$0 = (y + 9)(y - 2)$

Where the graphs meet, y is equal to 2 and 9

$y = 3x$ so the graphs meet when $x = 6$ and $x = 27$

Question 110: D

Working by orders of magnitude, multiply all the bacteria tested on the numerator and the number of resistances on the denominator. This gives an order of 10^{25}, which is the solution.

Question 111: B

Solve $y = x^2 - 3x + 4$ and $y - x = 1$ as (x, y).

Substitute the quadratic expression into the other non-quadratic. You will get another equation.

$x + 1 = x^2 - 3x + 4$

Rearrange to get a quadratic equation and solve.

$x^2 - 4x + 3 = 0$

$(x - 1)(x - 3) = 0$

Therefore $x = 1$ or $x = 3$

Substitute your x values into the equation, $y - x = 1$ and solve to work out y values.

$y = 2$ or $y = 4$

Therefore, the coordinates are $(1, 2)$ and $(3, 4)$

Question 112: C

Transform all numbers into fractions then follow the order of operations to simplify. Move the surds next to each other and evaluate systematically:

$$= \left(\left(\frac{6}{8} x \frac{7}{3}\right) \div \left(\frac{7}{5} x \frac{2}{6}\right) \right) x \frac{4}{10} x \frac{15}{100} x \frac{5}{100} x \frac{5}{25} x \pi x \left(\sqrt{e^2}\right) x e\pi^{-1}$$

$$= \left(\frac{42}{24} \div \frac{14}{30}\right) x \frac{4 \, x \, 3 \, x \, 25}{10 \, x \, 20 \, x \, 100 \, x \, 25} x \pi x \pi^{-1} x e^{-1} x e$$

$$= \left(\frac{21}{12} \div \frac{7}{15}\right) x \frac{12}{200 \, x \, 100} x \frac{\pi}{\pi} x \frac{e}{e}$$

$$= \left(\frac{21}{12} x \frac{15}{7}\right) x \frac{3}{50 \, x \, 100}$$

$$= \frac{45}{12} x \frac{3}{5000}$$

$$= \frac{9}{4} x \frac{1}{1000}$$

$$= \frac{9}{4000}$$

Question 113: B

There are several steps to working out this problem. The first is to work out the area of the entire floor, minus the fish tank and the cut out corner. We can see that the length of the room is 8m and the width of the room is 4m (the sides of the cut out square are 2m). Thus, the area of the entire room is **32m2**.

The cut out corner is a square with the dimension 2×2m. Thus, the area of the cut out corner is **4m2**.

The fish tank is a circle, and thus its area can be worked out using πr^2. П is taken to be 3 and thus $3 \times 1^2 = $ **3 m2**.

Therefore, the floor area, Bill needs to cover is $32 - (4 + 3) = 25$**m2**.

We then need to work out the area of one plank. The dimensions of this are in cm and so we need to convert to m. 1m is 100cm and so we can say that the length of the plank is 0.6m and the width is 0.1m. Thus, the area is $0.6 \times 0.1 = 0.06$**m2**.

To work out the number of planks, required, we need to divide the area of the floor space by the area of the plank. A quick way of doing this would be rounding the area of the room down to 24 and multiplying the area of the plank by 100 so it becomes 6.

$24/6 = 4$, then because we multiplied the area of the plank by 100, we then multiply the answer by 100 which gives us **400 planks.** The closest answer to our solution is 417, which is listed as B.

Question 114: A

$$\frac{(16x+11)}{(4x+5)} = 4y^2 + 2$$

$$16x + 11 = (4y^2 + 2)(4x + 5)$$

$$16x + 11 = 4x(4y^2 + 2) + 5(4y^2 + 2)$$

$$16x - 4x(4y^2 + 2) = 5(4y^2 + 2) - 11$$

$$x(16 - 4(4y^2 + 2) = 20y^2 - 1$$

$$X = \frac{20y^2 - 1}{[16 - 4(4y^2 + 2)]}$$

Question 115: B

Factoring the given expression will prove fruitless. Instead, identify its stationary points. Differentiating, we see that $f'(x) = 4(x^3 - 6x^2 + 11x - 6) = 4(x - 1)(x - 2)(x - 3)$, which we factorise by inspection (or by using the factor theorem). Now we can establish f(1), f(2), f(3), and using the asymptotic limits of $+\infty$ for both large positive and negative x, and the obvious root at 0, we have the following sketch., from which we see one positive root.

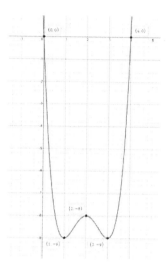

Question 116: A

We can factor the numerator as a difference of two squares $(\sqrt{x} + 2)(\sqrt{x} - 2)$, so we the integral is just $\int_0^1 1 - 2x^{\frac{1}{2}} dx = \left[x - 4x^{-\frac{1}{2}} \right]_0^1 = -3$

Question 117: A

In the first expansion, the coefficient of x^4 is given by $\binom{7}{4}3^4 b^3 = 2835 b^3$ and in the second, the coefficient of x^2 is $\binom{4}{2}(3b)^2 = 54 b^2$, and equating, we see that $b = \frac{54}{2835} = \frac{2}{105}$

Question 118: D

First calculate the equation of the tangent. By differentiating, we find $\frac{dy}{dx} = 2x + b$, and so at $x = 2, \frac{dy}{dx} = 4 + b$. The equation is this $y - (4 + 2b) = (4 + b)(x - 2)$ using the equation for a straight line though the point $(2, 4 + 2b)$. Now the x intercept is found by setting y = 0, and we find this to be at $\frac{4}{4+b}$. Now letting this be greater than 4, we find that $b < -3$

Question 119: B

Note that the inside of the bracket is a perfect square, and is simply $\left(3x + \frac{2}{x}\right)^2$. So $f(x) = 3x + \frac{2}{x}, f'(x) = 3 - \frac{2}{x^2}, f''(x) = \frac{4}{x^3}, f'''(x) = -\frac{12}{x^4}$, and so $f'''(2) = -\frac{3}{4}$

Question 120: C

We may factorise the function as $(x - 1)(x + 1)(x + 2)(x + 4)$, which allows us to graph it.

From the graph we can see that in the range provided by option C, $-2 < x < -1$, correctly describes some of the solutions to this equation.

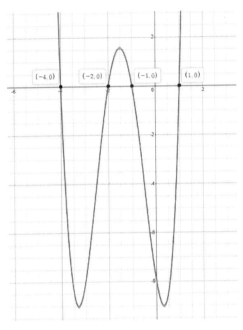

Question 121: A

Note $0.04 = \frac{1}{25}$. Consider the arithmetic series: $2 + 4 + 6 + \cdots + 2x = 2(1 + \cdots + x) = x(x + 1)$, so the exponent on the left is x(x+1)-2 So $5^{x(x+1)-2} = (5^{-2})^{-14} = 5^{28}$. Taking logs (to base 5): $x(x + 1) - 2 = 28$, giving $x^2 + x - 30 = 0$, which has positive root $x = 5$

Question 122: D

The easiest way to do this is by symmetry. If we have at most 2 heads, then we have at least 2 tails. If we swap the number of heads and tails, we now have at most 2 tails. So the question is symmetric in heads and tails, so the probability must be $\frac{1}{2}$

Question 123: E

We have an arithmetic progression, and $x_{100} = x_1 + 99q$, giving $q = \frac{1}{9}$. The sum to infinity is thus $\frac{a}{1-r} = \frac{5}{1-\frac{1}{9}} = \frac{45}{8}$

Question 124: B

The roots are given by $\frac{-3 \pm \sqrt{9 - 4(c-2)}}{2}$, making the difference $\sqrt{9 - 4(c - 2)} = 7$, gives $c = -8$

Question 125: D

The line of symmetry of $\sin(x)$ lie at $\frac{\pi}{2} + n\pi$, and so of $\sin(4x + \frac{\pi}{3})$ at $\frac{1}{4}\left(\frac{\pi}{2} + n\pi - \frac{\pi}{3}\right) = \frac{1}{4}\left(\frac{\pi}{6} + n\pi\right)$. Taking $n =$ 2 gives $\frac{13\pi}{24}$

Question 126: A

This is an example of the Collatz Conjecture. Applying the rule a few times we get the sequence 12, 6, 3, 10, 5, 16, 8, 4, 2, 1, 4, 2, 1... and we see it repeats. We see $x_8 = 4, x_9 = 2, x_{10} = 1$, and from then on x_n depends only on the remainder when n is divided by 3. Since the remainder is 1 when dividing 100 by 3, we see the answer is 1.

Question 127: E

Let $x = \sqrt{2}^y$. Substituting in gives $x^2 - 10x + 24 = 0 \rightarrow (x - 6)(x - 4) = 0$, so $x = 4, 6$. Now $x = 2^{\frac{y}{2}}$ and so $y = 2\log_2 x$, so the sum of roots is $2(\log_2 4 + \log_2 6) = 2(2 + \log_2 2 + \log_2 3) = 2(2 + 1 + \log_2 3) = 6 + 2\log_2 3$

Question 128: C

A good sketch will help.

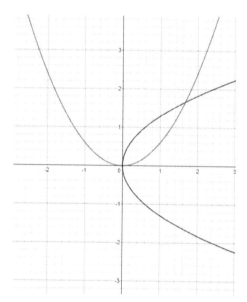

First find the intercept. At the intercept $x = py^2 = p(px^2)^2 = p^3 x^4$, and so $x(p^3 x^3 - 1) = 0$. Excluding the 0 solution, we see that $x = \frac{1}{p}$. Now we must compute the area, which is the difference of two integrals. We must invert $x = py^2$ to get $y = \sqrt{\frac{x}{p}}$, from which we compute the area as $\int_0^{1/p} \sqrt{\frac{x}{p}} - px^2 dx$, which one can compute to give $\frac{1}{3p^2}$.

Question 129: D

We can rewrite $\frac{x^2 + 2x}{\sqrt{x^3}}$ as $x^{\frac{1}{2}} + 2x^{-\frac{1}{2}}$. Now differentiating we get $\frac{1}{2}x^{-\frac{1}{2}} - x^{-\left(\frac{3}{2}\right)}$. We want this to be positive, ie $\frac{1}{2\sqrt{x}} - \frac{1}{x\sqrt{x}} > 0 \rightarrow \frac{1}{2} - \frac{1}{x} > 0 \rightarrow x > 2$

Question 130: C

The probability of any 3 given throws giving the same given number is $\left(\frac{1}{6}\right)^3$. Now any number can be repeated 3 times, giving us $\left(\frac{1}{6}\right)^3 \times 6$. Now we count the ways we can place these 3 throws in the 5 – this is just 5 choose 3, 10, giving $\left(\frac{1}{6}\right)^3 \times 6 \times 10 = \frac{10}{36}$. Now we have to discount the times that the other two numbers are the same as our given number. Fix a number n. The probability that in two throws, at least one of those yields n is just $\frac{11}{36}$, by counting the possibilities. (say n is 1, we get

11,12,13,14,15,16,21,31,41,51,61) for instance. So the probability it is not is $\frac{25}{36}$, which we multiply our previous probability by, so our answer is $\frac{10}{36} \times \frac{25}{36} = \frac{125}{648}$

Question 131: C

These are clearly circles. Completing the square on both gives equations of the circles $(x-2)^2 + (y-4)^2 = 8$ and $(x+2)^2 + (y+3)^2 = 3$, so we have centre (2,4) radius $2\sqrt{2}$, and centre (-2,-3) radius $\sqrt{3}$. The shortest distance clearly lies on the line between the two centres, which has length $\sqrt{4^2 + 7^2} = \sqrt{65}$. Now subtract the two radii. So the answer is $\sqrt{65} - 2\sqrt{2} - \sqrt{3}$

Question 132: C

Note that we may divide through by $\cos 2x$ to obtain the equation $\log x = \tan 2x$. We have to be careful though that we have no solutions when $\cos 2x = 0$, but this is clear since if $\cos 2x = 0$, then $\sin 2x = \pm 1$. Now draw a graph of $\log x$, and of $\tan 2x$ and count the number of intersections in the range. There are 5.

Question 133: E

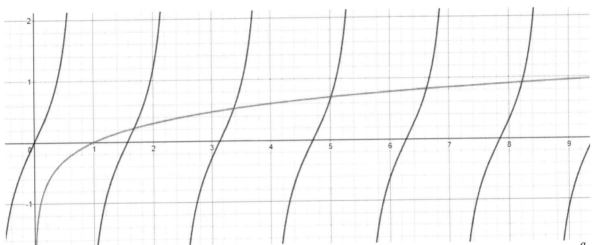

Let the first term of the GP be a and the ratio be r. We have a system of two equations in 2 unknowns: $\frac{a}{1-r} = 4$ and $\frac{a^2}{1-r^2} = 10$. We want to find r. Here's an approach. Rearrange the 2 equations as $a = 4(1-r)$ and $a^2 = 10(1-r^2)$. Divide the second by the first to get $a = \frac{10}{4} \frac{(1-r^2)}{1-r} = \frac{10}{4}(1+r)$. Now sub this back into our first equation to get $\frac{10}{4}(1+r) = 4(1-r) \rightarrow 10 + 10r = 16 - 16r \rightarrow r = \frac{6}{26} = \frac{3}{13}$

Question 134: B

If you know the chain rule, the integration is slightly less tedious, but if not, by expanding and then integrating we see that $V(t) = \frac{t^5}{5} + t^4 + 2t^3 + 2t^2 + t + c$. $V(1) = 5$ gives $c = -\frac{6}{5}$. Then $V(2) = \frac{236}{5}$

Question 135: B

$S_3 = 18 = 3a + 3d$, so $a + d = 6$, which is also $a = 6 - d$. We also know that $a + 4d = k$. Thus $3d = k - 6$, $d = \frac{k}{3} - 2$. The formula for $S_n = na + \frac{n(n-1)}{2}d = 6n - nd + \frac{n^2d}{2} - \frac{nd}{2} = 6n - \frac{nk}{3} + 2n + \frac{n^2k}{6} - n^2 - \frac{nk}{6} + n = 9n - \frac{nk}{3} + \frac{kn^2}{6} - n^2$ (using the substitutions of a and d).

This last expression has only two terms which might be non-integers, $\frac{nk}{3}$ and $\frac{kn^2}{6}$. To make the latter an integer for every value of n, k must be a multiple of 6, which also implies it is a multiple of 3. It is not necessary for k to have a factor of 18, as $k = 24$ works (common difference is 1, all terms integers which means all sums are integers). It is definitely not necessary for k to be odd as that contradicts it being a multiple of 6. Thus, the answer is I only.

Question 136: A

Using trigonometric identities, $\cos 2x = 1 - 2\sin^2 x$, $\sin 2x = 2\sin x \cos x$. This means that $\frac{\sin 2x}{1-\cos 2x} = \frac{\cos x}{\sin x}$. We then know the critical values of x are when $\cos x$ is equal to 0 ($x = \frac{n\pi}{2}$). The other part of the expression has only 1 critical value at $x = \log_3 2$. All that's left to determine is whether they are positive or negative around these values.

$(3^x - 2)$ is increasing, so it must be below the x-axis before $x = \log_3 2$ and positive after. We only need to consider $\frac{\pi}{2}$ which is the only critical value in range for this problem, and both $\sin x$ and $\cos x$ are positive at $x = 0$, so the graph must be positive before $x = \frac{\pi}{2}$ and negative after. We are looking for where they have the same sign, and we know that $\log_3 2 < 1$ (as $\log_3 3 = 1$) so it must be $\log_3 2 \le x \le \frac{\pi}{2}$.

Question 137: A

$25^{x-1} = 5^{2x-2} = \frac{(5^x)^2}{25}$ so, we make the substitution $y = 5^x$. This gives us $\frac{y^2}{25} + \frac{96}{25} = y$.

We can then immediately use the quadratic formula to get $y = \frac{1\pm\sqrt{1-4\times\frac{96}{25}}}{\frac{2}{25}} = \frac{25\pm\sqrt{25^2-24^2}}{2}$. Which means $y = 10 \; or \; y = 15$. i.e. $5^x = 10 \; or \; 5^x = 15$. $\log_5 10 = \log_5 5 + \log_5 2$ and $\log_5 15 = \log_5 5 + \log_5 3$ so the difference is $\log_5 3 - \log_5 2 = \log_5\left(\frac{3}{2}\right)$.

Question 138: B

To find an equidistant line, we must find the line which joins the two centres, take its midpoint, and find the line through it with the perpendicular gradient.

The circles can be rearranged to be $(y + 3)^2 + (x - 2)^2 + 12 - 9 - 4 = 0$: $(y + 3)^2 + (x - 2)^2 = 1$ and $(y - 1)^2 + x^2 = 9^2$. This means their centres are at $(2, -3)$ and $(0, 1)$. The joining line then has gradient $\frac{-3-1}{2-0} =$

~ 163 ~

-2, so its perpendicular has gradient $\frac{1}{2}$. We also know its midpoint is $\left(\frac{2+0}{2}, \frac{1-3}{2}\right) = (1, -1)$. Finally, the line must be $y + 1 = \frac{1}{2}(x - 1)$: $y = \frac{x}{2} - \frac{3}{2}$.

Question 139: B

To find the former, we follow the marble's path and calculate distances with Pythagoras. The first movement has distance $\sqrt{(7-4)^2 + (2-6)^2 + (12-0)^2} = \sqrt{9 + 16 + 144} = \sqrt{169} = 13$. The second movement has distance $\sqrt{81 + 169 + 25} = \sqrt{275} = 5\sqrt{11}$.

The overall distance is simply the distance form the first to the third point which is $\sqrt{144 + 81 + 49} = \sqrt{274}$.

The difference of the square of these distances is $\left(13 + 5\sqrt{11}\right)^2 - 274 = 169 + 130\sqrt{11} + 275 - 274 = 170 + 130\sqrt{11} = 10(17 + 13\sqrt{11})$.

Question 140: A

We must first find the stationary points. So, as usual we differentiate, set to 0 and solve for x. $f'(x) = 15x^2 - 5 = 0$ tells us that $x^2 = \frac{5}{15}$; $x = \pm\frac{1}{\sqrt{3}}$. To find the co-ordinates of the stationary points, we then find the corresponding y values. $f\left(\frac{1}{\sqrt{3}}\right) = \frac{5}{3\sqrt{3}} - \frac{5}{\sqrt{3}} + 6 = 6 - \frac{10}{3\sqrt{3}}$ and $f\left(\frac{-1}{\sqrt{3}}\right) = \frac{-5}{3\sqrt{3}} + \frac{5}{\sqrt{3}} + 6 = 6 + \frac{10}{3\sqrt{3}}$.

The distance between the 2 points is found via Pythagoras as distance $= \sqrt{\left(\frac{2}{\sqrt{3}}\right)^2 + \left(\frac{20}{3\sqrt{3}}\right)^2} = \frac{2}{\sqrt{3}}\sqrt{1 + \frac{100}{9}} = \frac{2\sqrt{109}}{3\sqrt{3}}$.

Question 141: B

Obviously, this question could be done by brute force, but there is a much quicker way. $301^5 = (1 + 3 \times 10^2)^5$. If we treat this like a binomial expansion, we are looking for the coefficient of 10^5. If we look at the first few terms, $(301)^5 = 1 + 5 \times 3 \times 10^2 + 10 \times 9 \times 10^4 + 10 \times 27 \times 10^6 + \cdots$. The later terms will be too large, and it is clear here the only 10^5 term here will have coefficient 9.

Question 142: D

The formula for x_{n+1} can be rewritten in the form $x_{n+1} = x_n^{-\frac{1}{2}}$. We can then say that $x_{n+2} = (x_{n+1})^{-\frac{1}{2}} = x_n^{\frac{1}{4}}$. What we have found is that $x_{n+k} = (x_n)^{\left(-\frac{1}{2}\right)^k}$. As we know that $1000 = 999 + 1$, $x_{1000} = (x_1)^{\frac{-1}{2^{999}}} = (10^3)^{-2^{-999}} = 10^{-3 \times 2^{-999}}$.

Question 143: A

We first determine what $f(x)$ is:

$(4x^2 - 7x + 1)(2x - q) = 8x^3 - 14x^2 + 2x - 4qx^2 + 7qx - q$

$f(x)$ divided by $(x + 2)$ is the same as $f(-2) = 8 \times -8 - (14 + 4q) \times 4 + (2 + 7q) \times (-2) - q = -31q - 124 = -31^2$. This gives us $q + 4 = 31$, so $q = 27$.

Question 144: A

With integrals with modulus signs in, we typically split the integral range into the parts where the modulus function is defined properly i.e. $\int_0^2 |x-1|(3\sqrt{x}-x\sqrt{x})dx = \int_0^1 (1-x)(3\sqrt{x}-x\sqrt{x})dx + \int_1^2 (x-1)(3\sqrt{x}-x\sqrt{x})dx$

You can notice here that the integrand is identical except for a minus sign in the 2 integrals on the right. This means we don't have to integrate two different functions, only 1, and change what we substitute in as limits.

If we take the first integral, $\int_0^1 (1-x)(3\sqrt{x}-x\sqrt{x})dx = \int_0^1 x^{\frac{5}{2}} - 4x^{\frac{3}{2}} + 3x^{\frac{1}{2}}\, dx = \left[\frac{2x^{\frac{7}{2}}}{7} - \frac{8x^{\frac{5}{2}}}{5} + 2x^{\frac{3}{2}}\right]_0^1$. But we then know that the second integral is just $\left[\frac{2x^{\frac{7}{2}}}{7} - \frac{8x^{\frac{5}{2}}}{5} + 2x^{\frac{3}{2}}\right]_2^1$. So, we simply calculate $2\left(\frac{2}{7} - \frac{8}{5} + 2\right) - \left(\frac{2\times 2^{\frac{7}{2}}}{7} - \frac{8\times 2^{\frac{5}{2}}}{5} + 2\times 2^{\frac{3}{2}}\right) = 2\left(\frac{24}{35}\right) + \sqrt{2}\left(\frac{4}{35}\right) = \frac{48+4\sqrt{2}}{35}$.

Question 145: B

The function is symmetric about 1, which means $\int_1^2 f(x)dx = \int_0^1 f(x)dx$. This implies that $\int_0^2 f(x)dx = 2\int_0^1 f(x)dx$. Making this substitution, we get a quadratic in $\int_0^1 f(x)dx$ with $\left(\int_0^1 f(x)dx\right)^2 + 4\int_0^1 f(x)dx - 12 = 0 = (\int_0^1 f(x)dx + 6)(\int_0^1 f(x)dx - 2)$. This gives us $\int_0^1 f(x)dx = \int_1^2 f(x)dx = 2$ or $\int_1^2 f(x)dx = -6$.

Question 146: A

This question relies on noticing the reason for not combining the constant terms inside each large square root. They are both in fact square numbers. The expression is equal to $\sqrt{\left(5-2\sqrt{5}\right)^2} + \sqrt{\left(\sqrt{5}-4\right)^2}$. As $\sqrt{}$ implies taking the positive root, we do have to determine whether these are positive or negative; $\sqrt{5} < \sqrt{9} = 3 < 4$, so it is clear that $4 - \sqrt{5} > 0$ but for the first, it is slightly closer. However, $2 < \sqrt{5}$ which means that $2\sqrt{5} < \left(\sqrt{5}\right)^2 = 5$, so $5 - 2\sqrt{5} > 0$. This means our sum is equal to $5 - 2\sqrt{5} + 4 - \sqrt{5} = 9 - 3\sqrt{5}$.

Question 147: D

Possibly the simplest way to consider this problem is to look at the number of patients who will survive. From splitting the wards up, we know that the number of patients who will survive is $\frac{3p}{5} + \frac{q}{9}$. We also know it is $\frac{p+q}{4}$ by taking the number of people in the whole hospital, and the overall survival rate. By rearranging the fractions, we get $108p + 20q = 45p + 45q;\ 63p = 25q; q = \frac{63p}{25}$. And q was the number we were looking for.

Question 148: C

The first thing to notice is these events are not mutually exclusive, so we cannot find their independent probabilities and multiply them. The easier to work with is the latter; the probability that we get 2 heads in the last three tosses is simply the probability the last three tosses come up as one of HHT, HTH or THH. Each of these is equally likely, with probability $\frac{1}{8}$, so the probability of this is $\frac{3}{8}$. If we know that both events occurred, then we must have gotten more than $(4-2) = 2$ heads in the first 4 tosses. This just means getting $2, 3$ or 4 heads in 4 tosses. Each sequence is equally likely (with probability $\frac{1}{16}$) and the sequences which we care about are $HHHH,$ $HHHT, HHTH, HTHH, THHH,$ $HHTT, HTTH, HTHT, TTHH, THTH, THHT$. There are 11 of these.

Now, with this event described as "getting more than 2 heads in the first 4 tosses and 2 in the last 3 tosses", the events are independent, because there is no dependence of any 1 toss on any other. This means we can multiply probabilities, and we get the answer to be $\frac{11}{16} \times \frac{3}{8} = \frac{33}{128}$.

Question 149: D

This is a problem about counting. The boxes are indistinguishable, which means we only care about how the balls are distributed, not specifically which boxes they are in.

A good way to approach these is to have an order to the counting. We shall do it based on how man boxes are empty at the end:

0 – This is only true if there is 1 ball in each box, and there is only one way to do this.   1

1 – There must be two balls in 1 box and 1 in the other 3. The two balls could both be blue, both be red, or be 1 of each.   3

2 – There are two possibilities here, a $3, 1, 1$ split, or a $2, 2, 1$ split. In the former case, the 3 balls could be all red, 2 red 1 blue, or all blue. Either way they uniquely determine the other balls. In the latter case, we consider where the two blue balls are; they could be in the same box, one could be in each of the boxes with 2 balls in, or one could be in a 2 box and the other in the 1 box. As there are no other ways to distribute the blue balls, this is an exhaustive list.   6

3 – All balls being only in 2 boxes means they are split $1, 4$ or $2, 3$. In the former, there are 2 possibilities, the single ball is red, or it is blue. In the latter, there are 3 possibilities for the box with two balls in, RR, BB or RB, but no matter what this also determines what is in the other box.   5

4 – Only one way, all the balls are in the same box.   1

Summing these possibilities, we have 16 ways.

Question 150: A

It is not strictly necessary to expand these brackets to find the answer to this question, however that is how we'll solve it. $\left(\frac{x}{2} + 1\right)^3 = \frac{x^3}{8} + \frac{3x^2}{4} + \frac{3x}{2} + 1$. $f'(x) = \frac{3x^2}{8} + \frac{3x}{2} + \frac{3}{2}$; $f''(x) = \frac{3x}{4} + \frac{3}{2}$. Then, to find $f''(2)$, we substitute in to get our answer; 3.

Question 151: C

Instead of trying to calculate sums involving 5^3, we can treat this like a factorisation problem. We are told that $(4x - 3)$ & $(x - 5)$ are the only roots, so we can deduce their powers in the factorisation of $f(x)$ by looking at the constant term. $75 = 5^2 \times 3$ which means our polynomial must be equal to $(4x - 3)(x - 5)^2$. From here, we can simply expand this and find our answer; $(4x - 3)(x - 5)^2 = (4x - 3)(x^2 - 10x + 25) = 4x^3 + 53x^2 + 58x - 75$. Then our average is $\frac{4+53+58}{3} = \frac{115}{3}$.

Question 152: D

We first differentiate the function, to get $f'(x) = 5ax^4 + 2x^3 + c$. We are told this at $x = 1; 5a + 2 + c = -a^2$.

Our integral can be found in terms of a and c as well; $\int_0^2 f(x)dx = \left[\frac{ax^6}{6} + \frac{x^5}{10} + \frac{cx^2}{2}\right]_0^2 = \frac{32a}{3} + \frac{32}{10} + 2c$. First of all, we can substitute for c to get $\int_0^2 f(x)dx = \frac{32a}{3} + \frac{32}{10} - 2a^2 - 10a - 4 = \frac{2a}{3} - \frac{4}{5} - 2a^2$.

This is a negative quadratic, so we can find its maximum point by completing the square. $\frac{2a}{3} - \frac{4}{5} - 2a^2 = -2\left(a^2 - \frac{a}{3} + \frac{2}{5}\right) = -2\left(\left(a - \frac{1}{6}\right)^2 - \frac{1}{36} + \frac{2}{5}\right)$. The maximum value of this is therefore $\left(\frac{2}{5} - \frac{1}{36}\right) \times -2 = \frac{67}{18}$.

Question 153: C

It cannot be $\frac{9+3\sqrt{6}}{2}$

These three terms must be of the form ar^n for some a and some r, with $n \leq 7$. The ratio between any two of them is $\frac{2}{3}$, which means $r = \frac{2}{3}$ or $r = \sqrt{\frac{2}{3}}$, as the terms could be consecutive or spaced two apart (they must be evenly spaced due to the ratio between $1:\frac{2}{3}$ and $\frac{2}{3}:\frac{4}{9}$ being equal).

If $r = \frac{2}{3}$, and if $a_0 = 1, S_\infty = \frac{1}{1-\frac{2}{3}} = 3$. But it may not start at 1. Starting at the term <u>before 1</u>, i.e. $\frac{3}{2}$, the sum would be $3 + \frac{3}{2} = \frac{9}{2}$, and another further back $S_\infty = \frac{9}{2} + \frac{9}{4} = \frac{27}{4}$.

Alternatively, if we consider the starting point of 1 with $r = \sqrt{\frac{2}{3}}$, $S_\infty = \frac{1}{1-\sqrt{\frac{2}{3}}} = \frac{\sqrt{3}}{\sqrt{3}-\sqrt{2}} = \frac{3+\sqrt{6}}{3-2} = 3 + \sqrt{6}$. If we consider starting at terms earlier than 1 as we did in the previous case, we must remember we can only take one step backwards before $\frac{4}{9}$ is the 7th term. Thus, $3 + \sqrt{6} + \sqrt{\frac{3}{2}}$ is a possible solution but $S_\infty = \frac{\frac{3}{2}}{1-\sqrt{\frac{2}{3}}} = \frac{3\sqrt{3}}{2\sqrt{3}-2\sqrt{2}} = \frac{3}{2}(3 + \sqrt{6}) = \frac{9+3\sqrt{6}}{2}$ is not a possible solution, as it would force $\frac{4}{9}$ to be the 8th term.

Question 154: A

The right-hand side can be converted, by combining the fractions, into $\frac{6}{1-\sin^2 t}$, which is $6\sec^2 t$. Then, by integrating, we get $x = 6\tan t + A$.

Using the initial condition, $A = -\frac{6}{\sqrt{3}}$. Then, substituting $x = 6\left(\sqrt{3} - \frac{1}{\sqrt{3}}\right)$ at $t = \frac{\pi}{3}$. This simplifies to $4\sqrt{3}$, by combining and rationalising the denominator.

Question 155: B

The time between 08:34 am and 11:12 am is 158 minutes. For each minute that passes, the minute hand turns an angle of $360 \div 60 = 6°$. Therefore, the total angle turned is 158 mins $\times 6° = 948°$, and the answer is B.

Question 156: D

The inflated football is spherical, so its volume is given by $\frac{4}{3}\pi r^3$ whilst the volume of the box containing the football is given by $(2r)^3 = 8r^3$. The ratio of the volume of the football to the volume of the box is therefore $\left(\frac{4}{3}\right)\pi r^3 : 8r^3$. This simplifies to $\frac{\pi}{6} : 1$, so the answer is D.

Question 157: D

First, the scaling factor between the similar triangles must be calculated which is given by 24 m $\div$ 14 m. The length of the base of the larger triangle, x, can then be calculated by multiplying the length of the smaller triangle's base by the scaling factor: 4 m $\times$ 24 m $\div$ 14 m. Therefore, $x = 96/14$ which is simplified to 48/7 or $6\frac{6}{7}$ m, so the answer is D.

Question 158: D

The external angle of a pentagon is 360 / 5 = 72 degrees, which means that the internal angle is 180 - 72 = 108 degrees. Drawing a line from point 4 to point 2 creates an isosceles triangle. The small opposite angles are therefore (180 - 108) / 2 = 36 degrees each. From point 4 to point 3 is due east (or 90 degrees), point 4 to 2 is 36 degrees less than this (90 - 36) = 54 degrees. To find the opposite bearing on a compass (point 2 to point 4) simply add 180 degrees to give 234 degrees. Therefore, the answer is D.

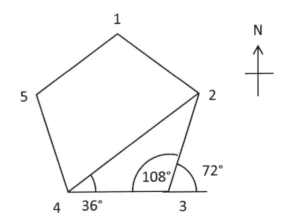

Question 159: C

First x must be found:

$$(7x)^2 = \left(3\sqrt{6}\right)^2 - \left(2\sqrt{10}\right)^2$$

$$7x = \sqrt{54 - 40}$$

$$x = \frac{\sqrt{14}}{7}$$

Thus, the triangles base is:

$$9x = \frac{9\sqrt{14}}{7}$$

Therefore, to calculate the area, use $\frac{1}{2} \times base \times height$:

$$= \frac{9\sqrt{14}}{7} \times 2\sqrt{10} \times \frac{1}{2}$$

$$= \frac{18\sqrt{140}}{14}$$

$$= \frac{9 \times \sqrt{4} \times \sqrt{35}}{7} = \frac{18\sqrt{35}}{7}$$

Therefore, C is the correct answer.

Question 160: B

First, the total area of the garden must be determined, and is calculated by 30 m × 20 m = 600 m². The total white space is then calculated by calculating the area of each of the white rectangles and adding them together. The area of the larger rectangle is 8 m × 10 m = 80 m², and the area of the smaller rectangle is (20 m − 8 m) × 4 m = 48 m². The area of the grey space is then determined by subtracting the white area from the total area: 600 m² − (80 m² + 48 m²) = 472 m². The number of rolls of grass is then determined by dividing the grey area by 10 m² (as the rolls are 1 m wide and 10 m long so the area of each roll is 10 m²): 472 m² ÷ 10 m² = 47.2. As it is not possible to buy 0.2 rolls, 47.2 must be rounded up. Therefore, 48 rolls are required to cover the garden, and the answer is B.

Question 161: B

There are (3 + 2) × 2 × 4 = 40 single shoes, half of which are left and half of which are right. After a left size 11 has been removed, there are 39 left. There are still 3 × 4 = 12 right size 11 shoes in the bag. Therefore, the probability of picking a size 11 right shoe is 12/39 and the answer is B.

Question 162: C

First, the surface area of a cylinder with radius 'r' and length '3r' is calculated by summing the surface area of each end and the middle section: $(2 \times \pi r^2) + (\pi \times 2r \times 3r) = 8\pi r^2$. The volume is given by the area of the cylinder end multiplied by the length: $(\pi \times r^2) \times 3r = 3\pi r^3$. Therefore, the surface area to volume ratio is $8\pi r^2 : 3\pi r^3$, which simplifies to $8 : 3r$. The answer is C.

Question 163: C

To find crossing points, we equate the two lines.

$$mx + c = (x-3)^2 - 4 = x^2 - 6x + 5$$

$$0 = x^2 - (m+6)x + 5 - c$$

The lines do not cross so there are no real solutions, thus $b^2 - 4ac < 0$ i.e. $(m+6)^2 - 20 + 4c = m^2 + 12m + 16 + 4c < 0$. We want the values of m which are at the edges of the interval which are $m = \frac{-12 \pm \sqrt{144 - 64 - 16c}}{2} = -6 \pm \sqrt{20 - 4c}$. Thus, the size of the interval is $R = 4\sqrt{5-c}$. Rearranging we get $c = 5 - \frac{R^2}{16}$.

Question 164: C

$f(1) = 0$ which means $(x-1)$ divides f. We can get the rest of the polynomial by long division or inspection from $3x^5 + 8x^4 + x^3 - 4x - 16 = (x-1)(ax^4 + bx^3 + cx^2 + dx + e)$.

By looking at the edge cases, $a = 3, e = 16$. Then $b - a = 8, c - b = 1$ and $d - c = -4$. From this we derive that $\frac{f(x)}{x-1} = g(x) = 3x^4 + 11x^3 + 12x^2 + 8x + 16$.

We then divide by $(x+2)$ in the same way, $3x^4 + 11x^3 + 12x^2 + 8x + 16 = (x+2)(ax^3 + bx^2 + cx + d)$ and again we find $a = 3, b + 2a = 11, c + 2b = 12, d + 2c = 8, 2d = 16$ to get $\frac{g(x)}{x-2} = h(x) = 3x^3 + 5x^2 + 2x + 8$.

Now, we are unsure what to do. However, knowing $f(a) = 0$ for some a does not mean it has only a simple root there. $h(-2) = 0$ still, so we can divide by $(x+2)$ again. By inspection, or the previous method, this is $\frac{h(x)}{x+2} = j(x) = 3x^2 - x + 4$. Checking the discriminant, $b^2 - 4ac = 1 - 48 < 0$ so this quadratic has no real roots.

Thus, 2 distinct real roots total, $x = 1, -2$.

Question 165: G

$S_5 = 5a_0 + 10d$ (by the formula for sum of an arithmetic series) and $a_{10} = a_0 + 9d$.

This means, in the case of I, $a_0 = -\frac{d}{4}$. This means that, whichever value a_0 has, the sequence will advance towards 0 initially. This means that, eventually, a_n will have the opposite sign to a_0, which means the product of this term and a_0 would be < 0.

In the case of II, $a_0 = \frac{d}{4}$. In this case and in case III, this means that the sequence progresses away from 0 at all times. Thus, if the sequence began negative, it would remain so, and vice versa.

So, the product of any two terms will always be positive. So, the answer is II & III.

Question 166: D

$(1 + 2kx)^2 = 1 + 4kx + 4k^2x^2$ is much smaller and easier to work with. If two of these coefficients are equal, either $1 = 4k \left(so\ k = \frac{1}{4} \right), 1 = 4k^2 \left(so\ k = \pm\frac{1}{2} \right) or\ 4k = 4k^2 (so\ k = 0\ or\ 1)$.

We must then only check these value in the expansion of $(k + x)^5 = k^5 + 5k^4x + 10k^3x^2 + 10k^2x^3 + 5kx^4 + x^5$. It is clear if $k = 0$ or $k = 1$ that there are equal coefficients here. If $k = \frac{1}{4}$, the coefficients are $\frac{1}{1024}, \frac{5}{256}, \frac{5}{32}, \frac{5}{8}, \frac{5}{4}$ and 1, of which no two are equal. If $k = \pm\frac{1}{2}$, the coefficients are $\pm\frac{1}{32}, \frac{5}{16}, \pm\frac{5}{4}, \frac{5}{2}, \pm\frac{5}{2}, 1$. It is clear that there is in fact an equality, but only for $k = \frac{1}{2}$. Thus, there are 3 valid values of k.

Question 167: D

We can rearrange this equation to $3^{\tan 2x} = \frac{1}{x}$, which can then be turned into $\tan 2x = -\log_3 x$. We can count the number of solutions by the number of intersections of the respective graphs of these functions. As a note, we know that the x-intersection of $y = -\log_3 x$ is before the intersection of $y = \tan 2x$ purely because the former is always 1, the latter must be $\frac{\pi}{2}$, and $\frac{\pi}{2} > \frac{3}{2} > 1$. This then has 3 solutions in the given range.

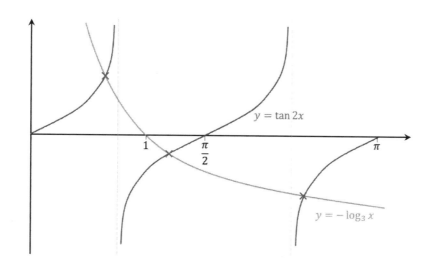

Question 168: C

Knowing that the highest point of $y = 5 - |x - 1|$ will be at $x = 1$ tells you that point is at $(1, 5)$, which is above the line $y = |x - 4|$ as it is at $(1, 3)$ there. This tells you there are two intersection points, with a quick sketch.

While this may or may not be to scale, it doesn't matter; we can see from the sketch that there is one intersection when both are in their first half, and one in their second half, whether the apex or base of either two graphs should be closer or further apart is irrelevant. Thus, we solve $5 - (x - 1) = x - 4$ (gives $x = 5$) and $5 + x - 1 = 4 - x$ (gives $x = 0$).

These points are $(5, 1)$ and $(0, 4)$ respectively and using Pythagoras' Theorem tells us their distance is $\sqrt{(5 - 0)^2 + (1 - 4)^2} = \sqrt{25 + 9} = \sqrt{34}$.

Question 169: A

The first integral will give us a relationship between a & b. We have that $\left[\frac{x^4}{4} + \frac{ax^3}{3} + \frac{bx^2}{2} + x\right]$ which must be evaluated at 4 (as at 0, it is 0). So, we have $64 + \frac{64a}{3} + 8b + 4 = 17 + \frac{16a}{3} + 2b = 0$ i.e. $b = -\frac{51+16a}{6}$.

We can then find the value of the 2nd integral in terms of a by evaluating our integrated expression at 3 and substituting for b.

We get $\frac{81}{4} + 9a - \frac{3}{4}(51 + 16a) + 3 = \frac{93}{4} - \frac{153}{4} - 3a = -3(a + 5)$. We don't even have to differentiate here, this decreases as a increases, which means we want the smallest a possible. As the question says that $a \leq 0$, this means we take $a = 0$ and get the integral to be -15.

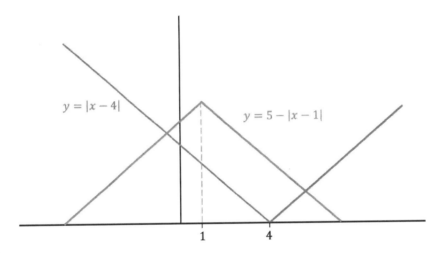

Question 170: D

$f(x) = \frac{x^4 - 2x + x^{-2}}{x^{\frac{1}{3}}} = x^{\frac{11}{3}} - 2x^{\frac{2}{3}} + x^{-\frac{7}{3}}$. Then, $f'(x) = \frac{11x^{\frac{8}{3}}}{3} - \frac{4x^{-\frac{1}{3}}}{3} - \frac{7x^{-\frac{10}{3}}}{3} = \frac{x^{\frac{2}{3}}}{3}[11x^2 - 4x^{-1} - 7x^{-4}]$. Thus, $abc + pqr = 11(-4)(-7) + 2(-1)(-4) = 316$.

Question 171: D

From the values given for the angles, we know that the angle at B is $45°$ or $135°$, and at C it is $60°$ or $120°$. This would imply at most 4 different triangles (if the length AB was not specified, it would be infinitely many as the size of the triangle wouldn't be specified), however we cannot be sure each exists. For example, if B and C take the larger values, the angles inside the triangle would sum to more than $180°$, which cannot occur. By drawing them out, with a side of fixed length and approximate angles at B and C, it can be seen the other three are all plausible. So, the answer is 3.

Question 172: D

Typically, it is good to find out whether each of the values you have is larger or smaller than some reference value. $1.4^2 = \frac{14^2}{100} = 1.96$, so perhaps 2 is a good reference value. $\sqrt{6} > \sqrt{4} = 2$; $\log_3 8 < \log_3 9 = 2$, $\frac{\sqrt{15}}{\sqrt{5}+1} < \frac{4}{\sqrt{5}+1} < \frac{4}{3} < 2$. And $\frac{13}{6}$ is just greater than $\frac{12}{6} = 2$. So, only two of our values are even greater than 2, so must only really compare them i.e. $\sqrt{6}$ and $\frac{13}{6}$. We can simply square both to see that $\left(\frac{13}{6}\right)^2 = \frac{169}{36} = 4 + \frac{25}{36} < 5 < 6 = \left(\sqrt{6}\right)^2$. So, as both are positive, we know $\sqrt{6}$ is the largest.

Question 173: C

It is first crucial to find the equation of l_2. It is perpendicular to l so has gradient -3, and we know it intersects l at $y = 8$. The x co-ordinate here is $3(8-3) = 15$. So, the equation of l_2 is $y - 8 = -3(x - 15)$.

We can now split the area we are calculating into two triangles and a rectangle; the rectangle will be the simplest, with opposing corners at $(0,0)$ and $(15,3)$. This lets our triangles be from the y-intersect of l to this corner to $(15,8)$, and from $(15,8)$ to $(15,0)$ to the x-intersect of l_2. These have respective areas $3 \times 15 = 45$, $15 \times \frac{8-3}{2} = \frac{75}{2}$ and $\frac{8}{2} \times \left(\frac{53}{3} - 15\right) = \frac{32}{3}$. The sum of these areas is our goal, which is $\frac{559}{6}$.

Question 174: B

$\log_8 xy = \frac{1}{2} = \log_8 x + \log_8 y$ We can then substitute for $\log_8 y$ in the 2nd equation to get $(\log_8 x)(\frac{1}{2} - \log_8 x) = -5 = -(\log_8 x)^2 + \frac{\log_8 x}{2}$. Making the substitution $z = \log_8 x$, we have a simple quadratic with solutions $z = \frac{-\frac{1}{2} \pm \sqrt{\frac{1}{4} + 20}}{2} = \frac{5}{2} \ or -2$. This gives us solutions for x of $8^{\frac{5}{2}}$ and 8^{-2}, which are $2^{\frac{15}{2}}$ and 2^{-6}.

Question 175: C

The volume of a cylinder of radius r, height h, is $\pi r^2 h$. The surface area is made up of two circles of area πr^2 each and the curved surface area, which is equivalent to a rectangle of side lengths h & $2\pi r$. Thus, from the question, we know that $2 \times (2\pi r^2 + 2\pi rh) \leq \pi r^2 h \leq 3 \times (2\pi r^2 + 2\pi rh)$. We can cancel some terms here which are positive to get $2 \times 2(r + h) \leq rh \leq 3 \times 2(r + h)$. By substituting in the value known for h, we know that $4(r + 8) \leq 8r \leq 6(r + 8)$. By splitting this up into two inequalities, we can get two conditions for r; $4(r + 8) \leq 8r$ implies that $32 \leq 4r; r \geq 8$ and $8r \leq 6(r + 8)$ implies that $2r \leq 48; r \leq 24$. These must both be true simultaneously so $8 \leq r \leq 24$.

Question 176: E

A tree diagram is very helpful in this situation.

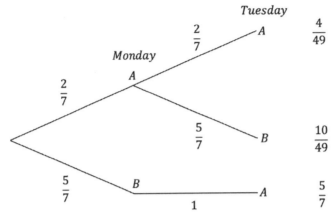

It can be seen that we have a $\frac{39}{49}$ chance of picking A on Tuesday. We also know we have a $\frac{4}{49}$ chance of picking A on Monday and picking it on Tuesday.

Because we know we picked A on Tuesday, we are only concerned with the outcomes AA and BA, as we know the other two did not occur. The probability that it was AA out of these two is then $\frac{P(AA)}{P(AA)+P(BA)} = \frac{\frac{4}{49}}{\frac{39}{49}} = \frac{4}{39}$.

Question 177: B

For the man to walk his dog "at least once every two days", we know he never had two consecutive days which he did not walk the dog. So, representing going for a walk as W, and not going as N, the possible ways he spent his 4 days are $WWWW, WWWN, WWNW, WNWW, NWWW, NWNW, NWWN, WNWN$. These are not all equally likely as each W has $\frac{1}{3}$ chance of appearing, and each N has a $\frac{2}{3}$ chance. Thus, the probability that each set of 4 days occurred is $\frac{1}{81}, \frac{2}{81}, \frac{2}{81}, \frac{2}{81}, \frac{2}{81}, \frac{4}{81}, \frac{4}{81}, \frac{4}{81}$. As we only want to know the probability any one of these occurred, we can sum them, to get $\frac{1+2\times4+3\times4}{81} = \frac{21}{81} = \frac{7}{27}$.

Question 178: E

This question is mostly an exercise in number manipulation. We first want to find out the area of the triangle. We would like to use $\frac{1}{2}ab \sin C$ but we have only one side length. It is easiest to first use the sine rule to calculate side length $BC = a$. This is then $\frac{a}{\sin 45} = \frac{500}{\sin 30}$; $a = 500\sqrt{2}mm$.

We can then use the cosine rule to calculate side length $AC = b$; $500^2 = 2 \times 500^2 + b^2 - 2 \times 500b\sqrt{2}\cos 30$; $0 = 500^2 + b^2 - 500b\sqrt{6}$. This is a quadratic for b, where we get $b = 250\sqrt{6} \pm \sqrt{6 \times 250^2 - 4 \times 250^2} = 250(\sqrt{6} \pm \sqrt{2})$. We know that the angle opposite this side is the largest angle in the triangle, so this must be the largest side, which means we take the positive root here. So, $b = 250(\sqrt{6} + \sqrt{2})$. We then use our formula for the area, to get area $= 250^2(\sqrt{6} + \sqrt{2})\sqrt{2} \times \sin 30 = 250^2(\sqrt{3} + 1)$.

Question 179: D

The length of an arc of a circle is simply $r\theta$ where θ is the angle in radians of the sector and r is the radius. We know the radius of this circle is 2, so the angle between the lines from the centre of the circle to the two points this line intersects the circle is $\theta = \frac{7\pi}{12}$. This may not seem helpful initially, however we also can deduce the angle between the y-axis and the radius to the one intersection point we already know.

The intersection is at $x = \sqrt{3}$, the it is at $\left(\sqrt{3}, 3\right)$ or $\left(\sqrt{3}, 1\right)$. It is the lower point so $\left(\sqrt{3}, 1\right)$. As the centre is on the y-axis, the angle a radius makes with the centre from this point is $\arctan\frac{\sqrt{3}}{1} = \frac{\pi}{3}$. So, the angle it must make on the other side of the y-axis is $\frac{7\pi}{12} - \frac{\pi}{3} = \frac{\pi}{4}$. This means the right triangle to the intersection point is isosceles, and the hypotenuse is still 2 (it is a radius) so the 2nd intersection is at $\left(-\sqrt{2}, 2 - \sqrt{2}\right)$. We can now calculate the equation of the line like any other, finding the gradient between the points and using one in the formula $y - y_1 = m(x - x_1)$. We get $y = \left(\sqrt{6} - \sqrt{3} + \sqrt{2} - 2\right)x - \sqrt{18} + 2 - \sqrt{6} + 3\sqrt{3}$.

Question 180: B

The first thing to do is expand this equation so we are working with a simple polynomial in t i.e. $\frac{dy}{dt} = 2t^{-3} + 3t^2 - t^4$.

We can immediately integrate both sides of this equation to get $y = -\frac{t^{-4}}{2} + t^3 - \frac{t^5}{5} + c$. Using the point we do know, we can substitute to find c. $2 = -\frac{1}{2} + 1 - \frac{1}{5} + c$; $c = 1 + \frac{1}{2} + \frac{1}{5} = \frac{17}{10}$. Then, we simply put this into our formula for y; $y = -\frac{t^{-4}}{2} + t^3 - \frac{t^5}{5} + \frac{17}{10}$.

Question 181: D

A stretch by a scale factor of 8 parallel to the x-axis is equivalent to the new function $\frac{\log_7 8x}{3}$. We are told this is the same as a translation in the y direction, which is equivalent to $\frac{\log_7 x}{3} + d$ for some value d. We can see that $\frac{\log_7 8x}{3} = \frac{1}{3}(\log_7 8 + \log_7 x)$. This means we have translated by $\frac{\log_7 8}{3} = \frac{3\log_7 2}{3} = \log_7 2$.

Question 182: D

The shortest distance between two lines is always a straight line, that must be perpendicular to both lines. This means that this "shortest distance line" for a circle must be an extension of a radius of the circle. Because we are comparing two circles, the shortest distance line is an extension of both of their radii; the only time these are the same line is on the line connecting the centres of the two circles.

We can complete the square on both equations to obtain $(x - 7)^2 + (y - 2)^2 = 3^2$ and $(x + 3)^2 + (y + 4)^2 = 5^2$. We can read off the centres of the 2 circles as $(7, 2)$ and $(-3, -4)$. We then need only calculate distance between these two points $\sqrt{(7 - (-3))^2 + (2 - (-4))^2} = \sqrt{100 + 36} = 2\sqrt{34}$. This value, minus the lengths of the 2 radii, is the distance between the two circles i.e. $2\sqrt{34} - 8$.

Question 183: B

The maximum straight line distance is from the front-bottom-left corner to the back-top-right corner (or another symmetrical orientation). The hypotenuse along the bottom face is calculated as $\sqrt{(3^2 + 4^2)} = 5$. The hypotenuse corresponding to the longest stick is $\sqrt{(5^2 + 5^2)} = \sqrt{50}$. This simplifies to $5\sqrt{2}$, and the answer is B.

Question 184: C

We first need to expand each bracket, giving:

$(2 - x)^2 = 2^2 + 2(2)(-x) + (-x)^2 = 4 - 4x + x^2$
$(2 + x)^4 = (2)^4 + 4(2)^3(x) + 6(2)^2(x)^2 + 4(2)(x)^3 + (x)^4 = 16 + 32x + 24x^2 + 8x^3 + x^4$
$(x - 2)^2 = (x)^2 + 2(x)(-2) + (-2)^2 = x^2 - 4x + 4$
$\rightarrow (2 - x)^2(2 + x)^4(x - 2)^2 = (4 - 4x + x^2)(16 + 32x + 24x^2 + 8x^3 + x^4)(x^2 - 4x + 4)$
$= (64 + 128x + 96x^2 + 32x^3 + 4x^4 - 64x - 128x^2 - 96x^3 - 32x^4 - 4x^5 + 16x^2 + 32x^3 + 24x^4 + 8x^5 + x^6)(x^2 - 4x + 4)$
$= (64 + 64x - 16x^2 - 32x^3 - 4x^4 + 4x^5 + x^6)(x^2 - 4x + 4)$

From the above, we can see that the x^3 term will be comprised of $(64x)(x^2) + (-16x^2)(-4x) + (-32x^3)(4) = 64x^3 + 64x^3 - 128x^3 = 0$

OR

We first need to realise that $(2 - x)^2 = \left(-(x - 2)\right)^2 = (x - 2)^2$. So:
$\rightarrow (2 - x)^2(2 + x)^4(x - 2)^2 = (2 - x)^4(2 + x)^4$
$= (2 - x)(2 + x)(2 - x)(2 + x)(2 - x)(2 + x)(2 - x)(2 + x)$
$= (2^2 - x^2)^4$

From the above expression, we know that **all x terms will have even power. Hence, x3 is zero.**

Question 185: A

$$\frac{1}{x^2+x-6} = \frac{1}{(x+3)(x-2)} = \frac{a}{(x+3)} + \frac{b}{(x-2)}$$

To find a and b, it is then:

$$ax - 2a + bx + 3b = 1;$$

$$a = -b \qquad (1)$$

$$3b - 2a = 1 \qquad (2)$$

Substitute (1) into (2):

$$3b - 2(-b) = 5b = 1 \,; b = 0.2 \to a = -0.2$$

Hence:

$$\int_3^4 \frac{1}{x^2+x-6} dx = \int_3^4 \left(\frac{-0.2}{x+3} + \frac{0.2}{x-2}\right) dx$$

$$= -0.2\ln(x+3) + 0.2\ln(x-2)]_3^4 = [-0.2\ln(7) + 0.2\ln(2)] - [-0.2\ln(6) + 0.2\ln(1)] = 0.2[\ln(2) + \ln(6) - \ln(7) - \ln(1)]$$

$$= 0.2\ln\left(\frac{2*6}{7*1}\right) = 0.2\ln\left(\frac{12}{7}\right)$$

Question 186: A

$$f'(x) = (-2)e^{-2x} + 2x$$

$$f''(x) = (-2)(-2)e^{-2x} + 2 = 4e^{-2x} + 2$$

Question 187: D

First, we need to find the gradient of the tangent:

$$m = \frac{dy}{dx} = 6x \,; \text{put } x = 1 \to m = 6$$

Equation of the line:

$$y - y_1 = m(x - x_1);$$

$$\to y - 3 = 6(x - 1)$$

$$\therefore y = 6x - 3$$

Question 188: C

Using division rule:

$$\frac{dy}{dx} = \frac{2(\cos(2x+5))(x^2+6x) - \sin(2x+5)(2x+6)}{(x^2+6x)^2}$$

Question 189: B

This is a geometric progression with first term 1 and common ratio ½ .

Hence: $S_\infty = \frac{a}{1-r} = \frac{1}{1-\frac{1}{2}} = 2$

Question 190: C

By factorisation, we can see that $x^3 - 7x + 6 = (x^2 + x - 6)(x - 1) = (x + 3)(x - 2)(x - 1)$.

The roots are then **x = -3, 2 and 1**

Question 191: B

$f'(x) = -2\sin x + 2x$

Question 192: A

$g = \frac{GM}{r^2}$; $g_{ground} = \frac{GM}{(6371x10^3)^2}$; $g_{top} = \frac{GM}{(7371x10^3)^2}$

$\frac{w_{top}}{w_{ground}} = \frac{g_{top}}{g_{ground}} = \frac{(6371x10^3)^2}{(7371x10^3)^2} = \frac{6371^2}{7371^2}$

Question 193: B

Kinetic energy = elastic potential energy

Maximum elastic energy $= \frac{1}{2}\frac{k}{2}L^2$; it's *k/2* because the springs are connected in parallel.

Kinetic energy $= \frac{1}{2}mv^2 = \frac{1}{2}\frac{k}{2}L^2$; $v = \sqrt{\frac{k}{2m}}L$

Question 194: B

For ideal gas, $PV = nRT$; pressure, moles and R are constant. Hence:

$\frac{V}{T} = constant$; $\frac{V_1}{T_1} = \frac{V_2}{T_2} \rightarrow V_2 = \frac{1}{2}V_1$; hence:

$\therefore T_2 = T_1 \frac{V_2}{V_1} = \frac{1}{2}T_1$

Question 195: E

Snell's law: $n_{air}\sin\theta_{air} = n_{water}\sin\theta_{water} = n_{oil}\sin\theta_{oil}$

You should know that $n_{air} = 1$. Hence:

$\theta_{oil} = \sin^{-1}\left(\frac{\sin\theta_{air}}{n_{oil}}\right) = \sin^{-1}\left(\frac{\sqrt{3}/2}{1.55}\right) \approx \sin^{-1}(0.56) \approx 34^o$

Ps. From all the options, 34° seems like the closest one. You should know that sin (30) = ½ .

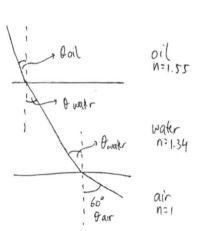

Question 196: A

We first need to find the gradient of the tangent:

$$m = \frac{dy}{dx} = \frac{1}{2}(8x - 4x^2)^{-\frac{1}{2}}(8 - 8x); \text{put } x = 2:$$

$$m = \frac{8-8(2)}{2\sqrt{8(2)-4(2)^2}} = \frac{-8}{2\sqrt{0}} \to \infty$$

From this, we know that the tangent is going to be a straight vertical line. Hence, the tangent is a line **x = 2**.

Question 197: B

Since $f(2x)$ is squashed horizontally, but we have scaled the integral by 2, we can immediately write down that $\int_1^3 f(x)dx = 1$. Now we are told that f is antisymettric in $\frac{3}{2}$. By drawing a diagram, it is easy to convince yourself that this is equivalent to $\int_1^2 f(x)dx = 0$. So then combining integration ranges we see $\int_2^3 f(x)dx = 1$, and so $\int_2^3 f(x) + 1\, dx = 2$

Question 198: C

Recall the definition of a prime – a positive integer whose only positive factors are itself and 1. I is false – 2 is a counterexample. II is false – 5 is a counterexample, it is prime and divisible by 5. III is true – no prime is divisible by 6, since then it must be divisible by both 2 and 3, neither of which can be p or 1.

Question 199: C

As $II \to III$, III is true. as $IV \to not\ III$ the contrapositive is $III \to not\ IV$ so IV is false. The contrapositive of the implication $Not\ I \to II$ is $Not\ II \to I$. But $Not\ II$ is false, so we can't say anything about I

Question 200: D

Of the list, 1 maxima and 1 minima is the only allowed configuration. For large magnitude of x, the graph looks like ax^7, so we must have an equal number of turning points of each kind.

Question 201: D

Given that the highest order of x in the first bracket is two, we see 3 different ways for an x^2 term to emerge:

A constant term from the first bracket, 1, multiplying an x^2 term from the second, $\binom{4}{3}\left(\frac{2}{x^2}\right)(-3x^2)^3 = -4 \times 2 \times 3^2 \times x^2 = -72x^2$

An x term from the first bracket, and an x from the second. This can't happen as in the second bracket all powers of x are even

An x^2 in the first bracket and a constant term in the second bracket. This gives $\binom{4}{2}\left(\frac{2}{x^2}\right)^2(-3x^2)^2 = 216x^2$

Putting this together we get a coefficient of 144.

Question 202: B

We have the two conditions $I \to II$, ie II *if* I, and $II \to I$, ie I *if* II. The contrapositive is equivalent to each, ie the first is equivalent to *not* $II \to$ *not* I, and the second to *not* $I \to$ *not* II. So B is not an equivalent formulation.

Question 203: D

Substitute the linear equation into the quadratic, to get an equation in x only: $x^2 - 16x + (32 + a) = 0$. Use the positivity of the discriminant to get the condition $32 \leq a$

Question 204: E

We need to count the number of multiples of two, but not of four, in the range. So 50,54,58,...98. There are 13.

Question 205: D

I is true, as we have just translated the function. II is true, as it is a stretch in x direction, translation and stretch in the y direction. III is false (can you come up with a counterexample?). IV is true – the equation holds exactly when $f(x) = 0$

Question 206: C

Expand the numerator, to get 4 terms as powers of x. Then differentiate. Either try to factorise the derivative – (noting $(4x + 1)^2$ must be a factor as it is in every answer), or expand the given answers. Doing so carefully gives the answer as C.

Question 207: F

This condition is convexity. You can see this by drawing a curve. At t=0 both the left hand side and right hand side are at x_1, and at t=1 both at x_2. The left hand side is just the function evaluated between x_1 and x_2, while the right is the value of the straight line between $(x_1, f(x_1)), (x_2, f(x_2))$, at the same x value as the left. The diagram below shows it is sufficient for the function to be curving up – ie $f''(x) \geq 0$

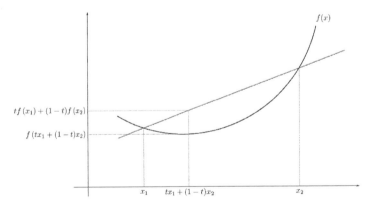

Question 208: C

The 6'th term can, with common ratio r, be written $ar^5 = \sqrt{32}r^5 = \frac{1}{32} \to r = \frac{1}{2\sqrt{2}}$. The sum to infinity is then

$\frac{a}{1-r} = \frac{\sqrt{32}}{1-\frac{1}{2\sqrt{2}}}$. This can be rationalised to $\frac{16+32\sqrt{2}}{7}$.

Question 209: C

Consider a set of 4 bulbs. Let 1 denote an on bulb and 0 an off. We start in 0000. Hit the second switch – 1010, now hit the 3rd – 1111. As 2020 is a multiple of 4 this strategy can turn on all the bulbs.

Question 210: B

We have an infinite number of geometric series. The sum of the first is $\frac{1}{1-\frac{1}{3}}$. The second is $\frac{\frac{1}{3}}{1-\frac{1}{3}}$... so the sum is

$$\frac{1}{1-\frac{1}{3}}\left(1 + \frac{1}{3} + \frac{1}{9} + \cdots\right) = \frac{1}{1-\frac{1}{3}} \times \frac{1}{1-\frac{1}{3}} = \frac{9}{4}$$

Question 211: E

The error is in cancelling the numerator at the start. The numerator could be 0. We can amend this by instead beginning by cross multiplying: $(2x^2 - 3x - 2)(x^2 - 5x + 6) = (x^2 + x + 1)(x^2 - 5x + 6)$, and so $(x^2 - 5x + 6)(x^2 + 2x - 3) = 0$, $(x - 3)(x - 2)(x + 3)(x - 1) = 0$, giving 4 solutions.

Question 212: D

Let's call $x = \sqrt{a - \sqrt{a - \sqrt{a - \cdots}}} = \frac{1}{a - \frac{1}{a - \frac{1}{a - \cdots}}}$, so that $x = \sqrt{a - x} = \frac{1}{a - x}$.

Now $x = \sqrt{a - x} \to x^2 = a - x$, and $x = \frac{1}{a-x} \to x^2 = ax - 1$. Combining these, we see that $ax - 1 = a - x \to x(a + 1) = (a + 1)$. a clearly isn't -1, so we can divide through and see $x = 1$. Substituting back into a previous equation we see that $a = 2$ is necessary. To establish sufficiency, we need to check they are indeed equal when a=2, but this is fairly obvious.

Question 213: E

I is true - $n^3 - n = n(n + 1)(n - 1)$ Any 3 consecutive numbers will always contain a multiple of two and three, so hence the product is divisible by 6. However, It doesn't have to be divisible by 4, for example n=6. III is true, because of I. You may worry about small numbers, (eg 5 is a prime, but is divisible by 5) but since 6 is not prime we don't run into issues.

Question 214: E

We can't compute the integrals (yet), so we resort to graphical methods. We know the immediately $B < A$ and $D < C$, since squaring a number less than 1 makes it smaller, and integration gives the area under the curve.

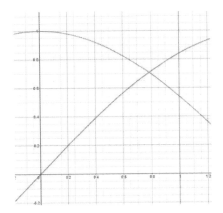

A good diagram clearly shows that the cos integral is larger than the sin, since the small triangle where sin is above cos is tiny compared to the section where cos is above sin: $A < C$. So now we have $B < A < C$, and just need to place D. One might suspect $D < B$ for the same reason as $A < C$. This is true:

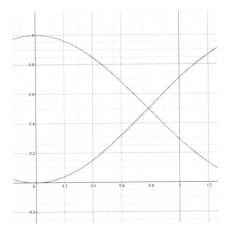

So we have $D < B < A < C$

Question 215: F

Begin by multiplying both sides by $\cos^2 3x$. This gives us $\sin^2 3x = \cos 3x$. Using $\sin^2 x + \cos^2 x = 1$, we can get a quadratic for $\cos 3x$ of $\cos^2 3x + \cos 3x - 1 = 0$. This has solutions $\cos 3x = \frac{-1 \pm \sqrt{5}}{2}$. However, $\cos y \geq -1$ for all values of y, which means only the positive root is taken. In the region 0 to 2π, we would normally have two solutions for any value of $\cos 3x = a$, so we have triple that amount in the case of $\cos 3x = a$, so we have 6 solutions.

Question 216: D

$4^{-6} = 2^{-12} = (2^3)^{-4} = 8^{-4}$, not 8^{-3}. So, line III.

Question 217: D

12 dividing a^2 does not imply that 12 divides a, take for example 6 squared. Thus, the error is in the line (IV).

Question 218: D

$f(r) = 0$ so $f(x) - f(r) = f(x)$ which means II is never true, as $f(x)$ has three roots.

$f(x + r)$ is a shift of the whole curve r units to the left. This does now guarantee that all of the roots of the graph are at $x \leq 0$, but if it had no <u>positive</u> roots to begin with, the curve does not now have fewer positive roots, so statement I is only sometimes true.

The original statement also did not say that the polynomial was cubic; while a cubic polynomial cannot have zero roots, a quartic polynomial, where one of the roots is repeated, can easily satisfy the original assumptions on $f(x)$.

And, it is also possible the other stationary point on this graph had a y co-ordinate between 0 and -1, which would mean $f(x) + 1$ would have no real roots. So, III is sometimes true.

In all, II is never true, I and III are sometimes true.

Question 219: G

If a decreases, then the graph will become flatter until the parabola turns upside down, thus I is possible.

II is not possible as b is not changing.

III is possible as despite changing, a and c do not have to change drastically, and without any markings on the graph a change in scale could make it look exactly the same.

IV is wrong as c must have decreased here, which it does not. So, it can't be II and IV.

Question 220: D

We need only consider terms which have x powers which sum to 3. The first bracket gives x^6, x^4, x^2 and constant terms, while the 2nd bracket has constant, x^{-1}, x^{-2}, x^{-3} and x^{-4} terms. The only combinations here which make x^3 terms are $x^6 \times x^{-3}$ and $x^4 \times x^{-1}$. The coefficient of the first is $1 \times \frac{4}{3^3} = \frac{4}{27}$ and the latter is $3 \times (-2) \times \frac{4}{3} = -\frac{24}{3}$. Taking the sum, we get that the coefficient of x^3 is $\frac{4}{27} - \frac{24}{3} = \frac{4-216}{27} = -\frac{212}{27}$.

Question 221: D

We seek a function which has 3 distinct roots and is not cubic. D. $(x - 1)^2(x - 2)(x - 3)$ satisfies this as its only roots are 1,2 & 3, but it is quartic. We need not consider any others.

Question 222: B

It is easy to check which of the roots are right by substituting into the original equation. We see that $x = 1$ is fine, but if $x = -2/9$, the right-hand side is less than 0, but the $\sqrt{x}$ symbol denotes taking the positive root. Thus, only $x = 1$ is correct. The error occurred in line (I) due to assuming no roots were generated from squaring both sides. This is what created the 2nd root.

Question 223: F

We want the two graphs to intersect but equating the expressions won't get us very far. Instead, a sketch of both graphs is more illuminating. The line intersects the y-axis at 10, which is much higher than the other line. The gradient of $\log_2 x$ is decreasing, and as the gradient of the straight line is constant, if it begins large enough, they will never meet. 10 is one such value and so anything larger will also never meet the curve. However, there are also slightly smaller values which would also work, so it is not necessary. For m negative, the line must proceed downwards from $(0, 10)$. One can see that, as eventually $\log_2 x = 10$, even an almost flat decreasing straight line would intersect the curve. Thus, no matter the value of m, if it is negative, the lines must cross. So, 1 is sufficient, 2 is neither.

Question 224: D

Usually, the easiest way to show a condition is "not necessary" is to find, or convince yourself you could find, a function which satisfies the condition that does not satisfy the alleged "necessary condition". However here, we know that $\int_0^1 f dx \leq 0$ because $x \leq 0$ for all the values of x we are considering. As $\int_{-1}^1 f dx = \int_0^1 f dx + \int_{-1}^0 f dx$, we also know that $\int_{-1}^0 f dx > 0$. This automatically satisfies D, for $a = -1$, so D is necessary, and we are only seeking one answer.

A is very nearly true, but any function which satisfies A actually has an integral of 0 from -1 to 1 (or from $-a$ to a for any a for that matter) because everything to the right of $x = 0$ perfectly cancels with that to the left.

For B, C and F consider the graph below. It has all the features of B,C and F, yet clearly the total area below the line is positive between -1 and 1.

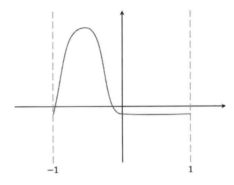

For E, this in fact can never be true, as it forces all x values everywhere to be ≤ 0.

The only condition left is D.

Question 225: F

We know that $f(x)$ is shaped roughly like the graphs shown. The 2nd graph is $f(x - b) - f(b)$, and the box in both graphs is the same size; it is $2b$ in length, and $f(b)$ in height. It is also clear to see that it encloses all of the area between the curve and the x-axis in the second picture. The excess being precisely what is described as R. Thus, the new area is $2bf(b) - R$.

Question 226: E

$\tan \theta$ has a root whenever $\theta = n\pi$ for some integer n. This means A has a root when $x = \frac{7n\pi}{5}$. Only one such integer n allows this to be in the given range, so $\tan \theta$ could be $f(x)$.

$\log x$ to any base always has 1 root at $x = 1$, and this is certainly in the range.

$\cos x = -1$ at precisely one point between 0 and 2π, at $x = \pi$, so $(\cos x) + 1$ has precisely one root. Similarly, for $(\sin x) - 1$, but at $x = \frac{\pi}{2}$.

3^x in fact, has no roots, anywhere, so cannot be $f(x)$ as it specifically has no roots in this range. So this is the answer.

Question 227: B

This is a relatively simple question if you pay very close attention, as the first error is in line I and if you spot it, you don't even need to check any other line due to the wording of the question. The question states "for non-negative n", but the base case checked is $n = 1$. This is not the smallest non-negative number, 0 is. In fact, for $n = 0$, this conjecture is false, as 6 is not divisible by 9. The answer is therefore line (I).

Question 228: F

In case I, two of the 5 keys were correct each time. This means that in total, 6 guesses were right. Each character was in a different position each time, which means the characters that were right in each guess were different. However, that would imply that 6 different characters were right, but there are only 5. This is a contradiction, so this could not have occurred.

In case II, it is possible, with the code *cbead*.

In case III, because none of c, d and e moved between the guesses, whether they were correct or not must have remained the same as well. This means that the number of characters which were correct out of a and b also remained the same. However, they swapped places, which means if they were both right, they are now both wrong (a change in the number of correct guesses by 2), and if one of them was right the other cannot be right when they swap (else both are correct for the same position, which changes the number of correct guesses by 1). We are left with the possibility they were both initially wrong, but in this case all of c, d, e are right in the first guess. This means the code can only be *abcde* or *bacde*. So, one of the two should have been 5, not 3. Thus, this cannot occur.

Answer: I and III can never occur.

Question 229: E

With integrals with modulus signs in, we typically split the integral range into the parts where the modulus function is defined properly i.e.

$$\int_0^7 |x - p| f(x) dx = \int_0^p (p - x) f(x) dx + \int_p^7 (x - p) f(x) dx$$

You can notice here that the integrand is identical except for a minus sign in the 2 integrals on the right. This means we don't have to integrate two different functions, only 1, and change what we substitute in as limits. By using the definition of F_1, we get $\int_0^7 |x - p| f(x) dx = F_1(7) - F_1(p) - F_1(p) + F_1(0) = F_1(0) + F_1(7) - 2F_1(p)$.

Question 230: C

If the cylinder encasing the sphere is as small as possible, the radii of the two must be the same (so the sphere is touching all of the curved surface area of the cylinder) and it must be touching both top and bottom circle caps of the cylinder. This forces $2r = h$.

The surface area is made up of two circles of area πr^2 each and the curved surface area, which is equivalent to a rectangle of side lengths h & $2\pi r$. Thus $B = 2\pi r^2 + 2\pi r h = 2\pi r(r + 2r) = 6\pi r^2$. We can rearrange this to find that $r = \sqrt{\frac{B}{6\pi}}$. We substitute this into the equation for the volume of S and get $V = \frac{4}{3}\pi \left(\frac{B}{6\pi}\right)^{\frac{3}{2}} = \frac{4\pi B^{\frac{3}{2}}}{3 \times (6\pi)^{\frac{3}{2}}} = \frac{B^{\frac{3}{2}}\sqrt{2}}{9\sqrt{3\pi}}$.

Question 231: D

A Venn diagram often helps in situations with probabilities which are not mutually exclusive.

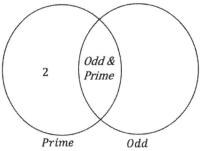

I is the same as the entire outside of the Venn diagram, but because the properties of being prime and being odd are not mutually exclusive, we cannot multiply them to obtain the probability they occur at the same time. So, this is not true unless the only prime number in the bag is 2, and we don't know whether this is true or not.

II is in fact the same statement as I, which is clear by looking at the Venn diagram. So, once again, as we do not know anything about the probability of picking 2 compared to an odd prime, we cannot determine this; it is not necessarily true.

III is the probability that the number picked is odd and not prime, which means it inhabits the "odd" circle in the diagram, minus the intersection. We know that the probability of being in this intersection is $P(\text{prime}) - P(2) = \frac{1}{5} - P(2)$. Thus, $P(\text{not prime and odd}) = \frac{1}{3} - \left(\frac{1}{5} - P(2)\right) = \frac{2}{15} + P(2)$.

Thus, only III is always true.

Question 232: D

As usual for surds questions, we can start by squaring both sides to obtain $px = x^2 + 2x\sqrt{p} + p;\ 0 = x^2 + \left(2\sqrt{p} - p\right)x + p$. This has exactly one solution so its discriminant must be 0 i.e. $\left(2\sqrt{p} - p\right)^2 - 4p = 0 = p^2 - 4p\sqrt{p} + 4p - 4p = p\left(p - 4\sqrt{p}\right) = p\sqrt{p}\left(\sqrt{p} - 4\right)$. This tells us there are two solutions; $\sqrt{p} = 0\ or\ 4; p = 0\ or\ p = 16$. 0 is obviously a valid solution, but 16 might not be, since we may have generated extra solutions. If we substitute in $p = 16$, we must solve the equation $4\sqrt{x} = x + 4; 0 = x - 4\sqrt{x} + 4 = \left(\sqrt{x} - 2\right)^2 = 0$. This has precisely one solution, so $p = 16$ is a valid solution as well.

We have 2 valid solutions for p.

Question 233: F

For I, the probability you get more than 4 heads in 10 tosses is the same as getting 6 or fewer tails in 10 tosses. But, as getting a head or tail is equally likely, this is also the same as getting 6 or fewer heads in 10 tosses.

Every possible outcome falls into one of these two events, which means that $P(\text{more than 4 heads}) + P(\text{fewer than 6 heads}) > 1$, and $P(\text{more than 4 heads}) + P(\text{fewer than 6 heads}) = 2P(\text{more than 4 heads})$. So, $2P(\text{more than 4 heads}) > 1$; $P(\text{more than 4 heads}) > \frac{1}{2}$.

For II, we know that the sequence we got appearing was one of the ways in which we could "get 7 tails", which means $P(\text{get 7 tails}) > P(\text{get our sequence}) = p$.

For III, the next 10 coin tosses are completely independent of any previous coin tosses we made. Which means the probability of getting this exact sequence this time, is exactly the same as the probability we were going to get it last time. So, it is still equal to p.

Thus, I and III only are right.

Question 234: D

Quartic equations only have an odd number of solutions if there is a stationary point on the line $y = 0$. So, we differentiate to find $x(4x^3 - 3x - 1)$. Setting this equal to 0, we find stationary points at $x = 0, 1, -\frac{1}{4}$. Then, we substitute into the original equation, and find we have $a = 0, -\frac{1}{2}$ and $-\frac{11}{2^8}$. This means these are the values of a for which the stationary point is a solution, and thus there are an odd number. i.e. sum of values is $-\frac{139}{2^8}$.

Question 235: B

Use the product rule $\frac{df(x)g(x)}{dx} = f(x)\frac{dg(x)}{dx} + g(x)\frac{df(x)}{dx}$;

with $f(x) = 5x^2$ and $g(x) = \sin 2x$ in this case;

hence $\frac{df(x)g(x)}{dx} = (5x^2)(2\cos 2x) + (\sin 2x)(10x) = 10x(x\cos 2x + \sin 2x)$.

Question 236: D

If $x = 1$ is a root, then *(x-1)* is a factor. Hence, factorise *(x-1)* out of the polynomial we get:

$(x - 1)(2x^2 + 3x - 2) = (x - 1)(2x - 1)(x + 2) = 0$

Hence, the other two roots are **x = ½ and x = -2.**

Question 237: B

Expanding this sum we get $3^{-0} + 3^{-1} + 3^{-2} + 3^{-3} + 3^{-4}$. This is a geometric progression with first term of 1 and common ratio 1/3. There are 5 terms in total, hence $S_5 = \frac{a(r^5-1)}{r-1} = \frac{1((1/3)^5-1)}{1/3-1} = \frac{121}{81}$

Question 238: A

$\frac{\log_2 8^x}{\log_3 9^y} = \frac{x\log_2 8}{y\log_3 9} = 12$; Hence $\frac{3x}{2y} = 12; \to x = 8y$. Substitute this into the 2nd equation:

$3(8y) + 5y = 10; \to y = \frac{10}{29}$ **and** $x = 8\left(\frac{10}{29}\right) = \frac{80}{29}$

Question 239: C

Take $3x^2 + 5 = u$; then $\frac{du}{dx} = 6x$. Substitute u and dx into the integral:

$\int_0^5 \frac{6x}{3x^2+5} dx = \int_0^5 \frac{1}{u} du = \ln u = [\ln(3x^2 + 5)]_0^5 = \ln(80) - \ln(5) = \ln(16)$

Question 240: C

First, we can see that this function has two roots, hence it is 2nd order polynomial;

$y = ax^2 + bx + c$

When $x = 0$:

$y = -8 = a(0)^2 + b(0) + c; \to c = -8$

When $x = 2$:

$0 = a(2)^2 + b(2) - 8; \to 4a + 2b = 8$ (1)

When $x = -2$;

$0 = a(-2)^2 + b(-2) - 8; \to 4a - 2b = 8$ (2)

(1) - (2):

$4b = 0; \to b = 0$

Hence **a = 2.** ➔ $y = ax^2 + bx + c = 2x^2 - 8$

Question 241: C

The x^6 term comes from $(x^2)(x^4)$ and $(x^3)(x^3)$ terms. Hence:

$$\rightarrow (3(1)(-2x)^2)(x^4) + (-2x)^3(4(2)(x)^3) = 12x^6 - 64x^6 = -52x^6$$

Question 242: C

$\log_4 \frac{1}{64} = \log_4 4^{-3} = -3$; hence $\log_3 x^2 - 3 = 3$

$\log_3 x^2 = 6$;

$x^2 = 3^6 = 729$;

$\therefore x = 27$

Question 243: B

$y = 5x^2 \tan(\frac{1}{2}x + 3)$;

Using product rule:

$\frac{dy}{dx} = (10x)\tan\left(\frac{1}{2}x + 3\right) + (5x^2)\left(\frac{1}{2}\sec^2\left(\frac{1}{2}x + 3\right)\right)$

$=10x \tan\left(\frac{1}{2}x + 3\right) + \frac{5}{2}x^2 \sec^2\left(\frac{1}{2}x + 3\right)$

Question 244: D

Line equation can be obtained by:

$y - y_1 = \left(\frac{y_2 - y_1}{x_2 - x_1}\right)(x - x_1)$

$\rightarrow y - 5 = \frac{-6-5}{2-(-3)}\left(x - (-3)\right) = -\frac{11}{5}(x + 3)$

$\therefore 5y + 11x = -8$

Question 245: D

This is an arithmetic series, with first term 1 and common difference +2. We first need to find the nth term of 99.

$99 = 1 + (n - 1)2$;

$n = 50$

$S_{50} = \frac{n}{2}(2a + (n - 1)b) = \frac{50}{2}(2 + 49 * 2) = 2500$

Question 246: E

The numbers have to be either 4 digits or 5 digits:

4 digits: 3xxx, 4xxx and 5xxx

5 digits: 1xxxx, 2xxxx, 3xxxx, 4xxxx, 5xxxx

3xxx = choose 3 digits from 4 possible number (1,2,4,5) → 4 x 3 x 2 = 24

4xxx = choose 3 digits from 4 possible number (1,2,3,5) → 4 x 3 x 2 = 24

5xxx = choose 3 digits from 4 possible number (1,2,3,4) → 4 x 3 x 2 = 24

1xxxx = choose 4 digits from 4 possible number (2,3,4,5) → 4 x 3 x 2 x 1 = 24

And so for 2xxxx, 3xxxx, 4xxxx and 5xxxx

∴ So total numbers are 24 x 8 = **192**

Question 247: E

$= (6\sin x)(3\sin x) - (9\cos x)(-2\cos x)$

$= 18\sin^2 x + 18\cos^2 x$

$= 18(\sin^2 x + \cos^2 x)$

$= 18$

Question 248: C

Define half the length of the inner equilateral triangle as x, and form a right-angled triangle by drawing a line from the centre of the inner circle to the inner triangle, defining the distance of that line as y.

$\tan 30 = \dfrac{r}{x}$

$x = \dfrac{r}{\frac{1}{\sqrt{3}}} = \sqrt{3}r$

$\sin 30 = \dfrac{r}{y}$

$y = \dfrac{r}{1/2} = 2r$

Using the formula for the area of a triangle, $Area = \frac{1}{2}ab\sin C$ in conjunction with the formula for area of a circle,

$Area = \pi r^2$, we know that: $Area\ of\ the\ small\ circle = \pi r^2$

$Area\ of\ the\ big\ circle = \pi(2r)^2 = 4\pi r^2$

$Area\ of\ the\ small\ triangle = \frac{1}{2}(2\sqrt{3}r)(2\sqrt{3}r)\sin 60 = 12\sqrt{3}\,r^2$

Therefore, the shaded area is: $Shaded\ area = (12\sqrt{3} - 4\pi + 3\sqrt{3} - \pi)r^2$

$= (15\sqrt{3} - 5\pi)r^2$

$= 5r^2(3\sqrt{3} - \pi)$

Question 249: A

$(3.12)^5 = (3 + 0.12)^5 = \left((3(1 + 0.04)\right)^5 = 3^5(1 + 0.04)^5$

$= 3^5(1 + 5(0.04) + 5\binom{4}{2}(0.04)^2 + \frac{5(4)(3)(0.04)^3}{6} + \cdots$

$= 3^5(1 + 0.20 + 0.016 + 0.00064)$

$3^5 \times 0.00064 = 0.16$. Therefore, I must obtain 4 terms in the expansion.

Question 250: B

$(\sin(\theta) + \sin(-\theta))(\cos(\theta) + \cos(-\theta))$

$= (\sin\theta + -\sin\theta)(\cos\theta + \cos\theta)$

$= 0(2\cos\theta) = 0$

Question 251: C

$(2x - 5)^2 > \left(3(2x + 1)\right)^2$

$(2x - 5) = \pm 3(2x + 1)$

Critical values: -2 and $\frac{1}{4}$ such that $(2x - 5)^2 > \left(3(2x + 1)\right)^2$ *within the range* $-2 < x < \frac{1}{4}$

Question 252: C

The distance between $(1, -4)$ and $(2,1)$ is $\sqrt{(2 - 1)^2 + \left(1 - (-4)\right)^2} = \sqrt{26}$. This is the radius of the circle.

The equation of the circle pre-reflection, therefore, is $(x - 2)^2 + (y - 1)^2 = 26$.
Upon reflection in the line $y = x$, the x and y coordinates of the circle change places, but the radius remains the same. Thus, the equation of the circle becomes $(x - 1)^2 + (y - 2)^2 = 26$.

Question 253: D

Since the new computer does a calculation in b hours, it does $\frac{a}{60b}$ calculations in one minute. Simply add the individual rates together and multiply their sum by m minutes total to receive: $m\left(\frac{a}{60b} + \frac{c}{d}\right)$.

Question 254: D

Since -1 is a zero of the function, $(x + 1)$ is a factor of the overall polynomial. By long division or synthetic division, we can determine that $\frac{2x^3 + 3x^2 - 20x - 21}{x + 1} = 2x^2 + x - 21$.
Factoring $2x^2 + x - 21 = 0$, we get: $(2x + 7)(x - 3) = 0$

The roots are $x = -\frac{7}{2}$ or $x = 3$.

Question 255: D

From these roots, we can find the factor of the polynomial:

$(x + 1)(x)(x - 1) = 0$

Opening the bracket gives us:

$f(x) = (x + 1)(x)(x - 1) = (x^2 + x)(x - 1) = (x^3 - x^2 + x^2 - x) = x^3 - x$

Question 256: A

The expansion of $y_1 = (1 - x)^6 = 1 - 6x + 15x^2$
The expansion of $y_2 = (1 + 2x)^6 = 1 + 12x + 60x^2$
The ratio of the second coefficient of y_1 to the third coefficient of y_2 is $-\frac{6}{60} = -\frac{1}{10}$.

Question 257: C

These integers form an arithmetic progression with 300 terms, where n = 300, $a_1 = 1$, and $a_n = 300$. If you substitute these values into the formula for the sum of a finite arithmetic sequence, you will get:
$S_n = 1 + 2 + 3 + 4 + 5 + \cdots + 300$
$S_n = \frac{n}{2}(a_1 + a_n)$
$S_n = \frac{300}{2}(1 + 300)$
$S_n = 150(301) = 45150$

Question 258: D

Recall the double angle formula for sine: $\sin 2\theta = 2\sin\theta\cos\theta$

Since $\sin 2\theta = \frac{2}{5}$, $2\sin\theta\cos\theta = \frac{2}{5}$, $\sin\theta\cos\theta = \frac{1}{5}$

$\frac{1}{\sin\theta\cos\theta} = \left(\frac{1}{\frac{1}{5}}\right) = 5$

Question 259: D

$-11 + 4\lfloor n \rfloor = 5$
$4\lfloor n \rfloor = 16$
$\lfloor n \rfloor = 4$
Since 4 is the greatest integer less than or equal to n, n must be on the interval $4 \le n < 5$.

Question 260: B

$\left(\frac{T}{4\pi}\right)^2 = \frac{l(M + 3m)}{3g(M + 2m)}$

$\frac{T^2}{16\pi^2} \times \frac{3g}{l} = \frac{M + 3m}{M + 2m}$

$3gT^2(M + 2m) = 16l\pi^2(M + 3m)$

$3gT^2M + 6gT^2m = 16l\pi^2M + 48l\pi^2m$

$6gT^2m - 48l\pi^2m = 16l\pi^2M - 3gT^2M$

$m(6gT^2 - 48l\pi^2) = 16l\pi^2M - 3gT^2M$

$m = \frac{16l\pi^2M - 3gT^2M}{6gT^2 - 48l\pi^2}$

Question 261: B

First, we set the two equations equal to one another: $k(x + 4) = 8 - 4x - 2x^2$

$2x^2 + kx + 4x + 4k - 8 = 0$
$2x^2 + (k + 4)x + 4(k - 2) = 0$

Subsequently, we set $b^2 - 4ac = 0$, as follows: $(k + 4)^2 - 4 \times 2 \times 4(k - 2) = 0$

$k^2 - 24k + 80 = 0$

Solving this equation yields: $k = 4, k = 20$

Question 262: A

We can find the common ratio of the series by dividing the second term of the series by the first, yielding the common ratio $r = \left(-\frac{1}{2}\right)x$

Since we know that the fifth coefficient is equivalent to $\frac{1}{32}$, we can solve for the value of x, the first term in the series, by equating 1/32 to the formula for the fifth term of a geometric series:

$\frac{1}{32} = ar^4$

$\frac{1}{32} = x\left(\left(-\frac{1}{2}\right)x\right)^4$

$\frac{1}{32} = \left(\frac{1}{16}\right)x^5$

$x^5 = \left(\frac{16}{32}\right)$

$x = \frac{(16)^{\left(\frac{1}{5}\right)}}{2}$

This is an infinite geometric series with a first term of $a = x = \frac{(16)^{\left(\frac{1}{5}\right)}}{2}$. We can simply find the common ratio by substituting $r = \left(-\frac{1}{2}\right)x = \left(-\frac{1}{2}\right)\frac{(16)^{\left(\frac{1}{5}\right)}}{2}$.

The sum to infinity of a geometric series is given by $S_\infty = \frac{a}{1-r}$. Therefore, the sum of the series is given by:

$$S_\infty = \frac{\left(\frac{16^{\frac{1}{5}}}{2}\right)}{1-(-\frac{1}{2})\left(\frac{(16)^{\left(\frac{1}{5}\right)}}{2}\right)}$$

$$S_\infty = \frac{16^{\frac{1}{5}}}{2+\frac{(16^{\frac{1}{5}})}{2}}$$

Question 263: D

$\log_2 3 \times \frac{\log_2 4}{\log_2 3} \times \frac{\log_2 5}{\log_2 4} \cdots \frac{\log_2 (n+1)}{\log_2 n} \leq 10$

Solving the above equation, we have that $\log_2(n + 1) \leq 10$. Consequently, $n + 1 \leq 1024$. The largest value of n that satisfies this equation is 1023.

Question 264: B

We have:
$(a + b + c)^2 = a^2 + b^2 + c^2 + 2(ab + bc + ca) = 364 + 2(ab + bc + ca) = 26^2 = 676$
so $ab + bc + ca = 156$.
Since b and c are the second and third terms of a geometric progression respectively, let us denote $b = ar$, and $c = ar^2$
We have $a + b + c = a + ar + ar^2 = 26$ and $ab + bc + ca = a^2r + a^2r^3 + a^2r^2 = 156$
$a(1 + r + r^2) = 26$ and $a^2r(1 + r + r^2) = 156 = 6 \cdot 26$.

We can divide both equations to get
$a^2r(1 + r + r2)/a(1 + r + r^2) = 6$, or $ar = b = 6$.

Question 265: A

$f(x)$ is a parabola, which is opened up (since its leading coefficient is $a^2 + 1 > 0$), so it has only one extremum and it is a global minimum. $f'(x) = 0 <=> 2(a^2 + 1)x - 2a = 0$, or $x = \frac{a}{a^2+1}$. Luckily for us, $\frac{a}{a^2+1} = \frac{1}{2} \times \frac{2a}{a^2+1} \leq 1/2$
(since $0 \leq \frac{2a}{a^2+1} \leq 1$ for any positive a).
As a result, the minimum in the interval is reached for $x = \frac{a}{a^2+1}$.

We substitute into *f(x)* to reach
$$fmin(x) = f\left(\frac{a}{a^2+1}\right) = (a^2 + 1).\left(\frac{a}{a^2+1}\right)^2 - 2a \times \frac{a}{a^2+1} + 10$$

$$= \frac{a^2}{a^2+1} - \frac{2a^2}{a^2+1} + 10 = 10 - \frac{a^2}{a^2+1} = \frac{9a^2+10}{a^2+1}$$

We want this value to be equal to $\frac{451}{50}$.
$\frac{9a^2+10}{a^2+1} = \frac{451}{50}$, so we cross multiply: $450a^2 + 500 = 451a^2 + 451$, or $a^2 = 49$.

Which means that $a = 7$, since $a > 0$.

Question 266: B

We know that rain and snow are independent events. If the probability that it will rain is $\frac{2}{3}$ and the probability that it will both rain and snow the following day is $\frac{1}{5}$, we can find the probability that it will snow the day after tomorrow by simply solving the equation: $\frac{2}{3}x = \frac{1}{5}$

Which yields: $x = \frac{3}{10}$

Question 267: A

Let us use the double angle formula, $\cos 2\theta = \cos^2\theta - \sin^2\theta$.

Given we know that $\cos 2\theta = \frac{3}{4} = \cos^2\theta - \sin^2\theta$, we know that $\frac{1}{\cos^2\theta - \sin^2\theta} = \frac{1}{\frac{3}{4}} = \frac{4}{3}$.

Question 268: B

If you draw the graphs, you will notice that the two graphs are the reflections of one another in the y-axis.

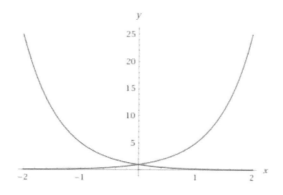

Question 269: C

Note that $1 = \log_4(4)$.

$\log_4(2x + 3) + \log_4(2x + 15) - \log_4(4) = \log_4(14x + 5)$
$\log_4(2x + 3)(2x + 15) = \log_4 4(14x + 5)$
$(2x + 3)(2x + 15) = 56x + 20$
$4x^2 + 36x + 45 = 56x + 20$
$4x^2 - 20x + 25 = 0$
By factoring,
$4x^2 - 20x + 25 = 0$
$(2x - 5)^2 = 0$

Hence, $x = \dfrac{5}{2}$

Question 270: E

Begin by subtracting the integral from both sides producing $x - \int_{-z}^{z} 9a - 7 = \dfrac{\sqrt{b^3 - 9st}}{13j}$. Next multiply both sides by $13j$ and square, rendering $[13j(x - \int_{-z}^{z} 9a - 7)]^2 = b^3 - 9st$. Finally subtract b^3 from both sides and divide by $-9s$ leaving the correct answer: $\dfrac{[13j(x - \int_{-z}^{z} 9a - 7)]^2 - b^3}{-9s} = t$.

Question 271: E

In order to start rearranging the fraction begin by adding m to both sides and squaring to yield

$$4m^2 = \frac{9xy^3z^5}{3x^9yz^4}$$

Now it is clear to see that this can be most simply displayed in terms of powers. Therefore, E is the correct answer

Question 272: A

The gradient of the curve is $\frac{dy}{dx} = 2e^{2x-5}$. We know that the gradient of the normal to the curve is $-\frac{1}{\frac{dy}{dx}}$.

Consequently, the equation of the normal is $y - e^{-1} = -\frac{e}{2}(x - 2)$.

At the point A, where $y = 0$, $x = 2 + \left(\frac{2}{e^2}\right)$

At point B, where x=0, $y = e + \frac{1}{e} = \frac{e^2+1}{e}$

Since the area of a triangle is $\frac{1}{2} \times Base \times Height$, the area of the triangle OAB is:

$$Area = \frac{1}{2} \times \frac{e^2+1}{e} \times 2 \times \frac{1+e^2}{e^2} = \frac{(e^2+1)^2}{e^3}$$

Question 273: D

We know that $(sec\ x + tan\ x)(sec\ x - tan\ x) = sec^2 x - tan^2 x$.

Using the trigonometric identity $sec^2 x - tan^2 x = 1$, as well as the information provided in the question, we know that:

$-5(sec\ x + tan\ x) = 1$

Therefore,

$(sec\ x + tan\ x) = -\frac{1}{5}$

By substitution, we know that $sec\ x - tan\ x + (sec\ x + tan\ x) = -5 + \left(-\frac{1}{5}\right)$

$2\ sec\ x = -5.2$

$sec\ x = -\frac{5.2}{2} = -2.6 = -\frac{13}{5}$

Since $sec\ x = \frac{1}{cos\ x}$,

$cos\ x = \frac{1}{sec\ x} = -\frac{5}{13}$

Question 274: B

First, let us find the points along which any potential intersection between the line and the curve would take place, by setting the two equations equal to one another.

$x^2 + (3k - 4)x + 13 = 2x + k$

$x^2 + 3kx - 6x + 13 - k = 0$

$x^2 + 3(k - 2)x + 13 - k = 0$

Since the line and the curve do not intersect, we know that there must not be any real roots.

As such, by the discriminant condition, we know that $b^2 - 4ac < 0$.

Therefore:

$(3(k - 2))^2 - 4(13 - k) < 0$

$9(k^2 - 4k + 4) - 52 + 4k < 0$

$9k^2 - 32k - 16 < 0$

$(9k + 4)(k - 4)$

We know that the critical values therefore extend from $-\frac{4}{9} < k < 4$.

Question 275: A

The distance AC (equivalent to the radius of the circle) can be determined given the coordinates of A and C:

$A = (-2,1)\ C = (5,-3)$

Therefore $AC = \sqrt{(5 + 2)^2 + (1 + 3)^2} = \sqrt{65}$

To find the length of the line CT, we use Pythagoras' Theorem:

$CT^2 = AT^2 + AC^2$

$CT^2 = 4^2 + 65$

$CT^2 = 81$

$CT = 9$

Question 276: B

At the stationary point, $\frac{dy}{dx} = 0$. Using the product rule: $\frac{dy}{dx} = x^2 e^x + e^x \times 2x$

When $\frac{dy}{dx} = 0$, $x^2 e^x + e^x \times 2x = 0$

Hence, $xe^x(x + 2) = 0$

Which shows that the x-coordinates passing through the stationary points of $y = x^2 e^x$ are x=0 and x= -2 respectively. Therefore, the equation of the quadratic function is: $x(x + 2) = x^2 + 2x$.

Question 277: B

The numerator of $\frac{x^2-16}{x^2-4x}$ is in the form $a^2 - b^2$, which means that it can be expressed as the quantity $(a + b)(a - b) = (x + 4)(x - 4)$

In turn, the numerator can be simplified into: $x(x - 4)$.

$\frac{x^2-16}{x^2-4x}$ can therefore be expressed as: $\frac{(x+4)(x-4)}{x(x-4)}$

Which simplifies to: $\frac{(x+4)}{x}$

Question 278: B

We can use the inclusion-exclusion principle to find the probability that none of the balls are red. Since there are 2n blue balls, n red balls, and 3n balls altogether, the probability of drawing no red balls within the two draws is: $\frac{2n}{3n} \times \frac{(2n-1)}{(3n-1)} = \frac{4n-2}{3(3n-1)}$

Therefore, the probability of drawing at least one red ball is equal to:

$1 - \frac{4n-2}{3(3n-1)} = \frac{3(3n-1)-(4n-2)}{3(3n-1)} = \frac{9n-3-4n+2}{3(3n-1)} = \frac{5n-1}{3(3n-1)}$

Question 279: A

Recall the discriminant condition for the existence of real and distinct roots,
$b^2 - 4ac > 0$

Using the coefficients in our question, this is: $(a - 2)^2 > 4a(-2)$
$a^2 + 4a + 4 > 0$
$(a + 2)^2 > 0$
Since this is a squared number, all values **but** $a = -2$ will satisfy this equation.

Question 280: D

Let $y = 2^x$. Then, $y^2 - 8y + 15 = 0$.

Solving this either using the quadratic equation or otherwise, we obtain y = 3 or y = 5.
If $3 = 2^x \rightarrow x = log_2 3 = \frac{log_{10} 3}{log_{10} 2}$

If $5 = 2^x \rightarrow x = \frac{log_{10} 5}{log_{10} 2}$.

The sum of the roots is $\frac{log_{10} 3}{log_{10} 2} + \frac{log_{10} 5}{log_{10} 2} = \frac{log_{10}(3*5)}{log_{10} 2} = \frac{log_{10} 15}{log_{10} 2}$

Question 281: C

Take logs of each side and separate out the LHS:
$3x \, log_{10} a + x \, log_{10} b + 4x \, log_{10} c = log_{10} 2$
$x \, (3 \, log_{10} a + log_{10} b + 4 \, log_{10} c) = log_{10} 2$
$x \, log_{10}(a^3 bc^4) = log_{10} 2$
$x = \frac{log_{10} 2}{log_{10}(a^3 bc^4)}$

Question 282: B

Algebraically, we can find the result of reflecting the curve $y = x^2 + 3$ across the line y=x by replacing y with x in the equation, and solving for the value of y in order to find the relevant equation, which is:

$x = f(y) = \sqrt{y - 3}$

Replacing y with x gives:

$y = \sqrt{x - 3}$

Translating the resulting equation by $\binom{4}{2}$ corresponds to introducing (-4) to the x term and (+2) to the y:

$y + 2 = \sqrt{x - 4 - 3}$

$y = \sqrt{x - 7} + 2$

The x-intercept is found by setting f(x) = 0.

$$\sqrt{x-7}+2=0$$
$$\sqrt{x-7}=-2$$
$$x-7=4$$
$$x=11$$

Question 283: C

Segment area $=\frac{60}{360}\pi r^2=\frac{1}{6}\pi r^2$

$\frac{x}{\sin 30°}=\frac{2r}{\sin 60°}$
$\frac{2r}{\sqrt{3}}$

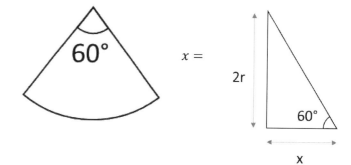

Total triangle area $= 2\times\frac{1}{2}\times\frac{2r}{\sqrt{3}}\times 2r=\frac{4r^2}{\sqrt{3}}$

Proportion covered: $\dfrac{\frac{1}{6}\pi r^2}{\frac{4r^2}{\sqrt{3}}}=\frac{\sqrt{3}\pi}{24}\approx 23\%$

Question 284: B

$(2r)^2=r^2+x^2$

$3r^2=x^2$

$x=\sqrt{3}r$

$Total\ height\ =\ 2r+x=(2+\sqrt{3})r$

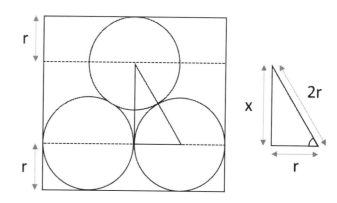

Question 285: A

$V=\frac{1}{3}h\times \text{base area}$

Therefore base area must be equal if h and V are the same

Internal angle $= 180° -$ external ; external $= 360°/6 = 60°$ giving internal angle $120°$

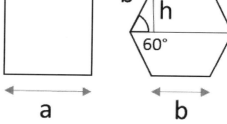

Hexagon is two trapezia of height h where: $\frac{b}{\sin 90°}=\frac{h}{\sin 60°}$

$h=\frac{\sqrt{3}}{2}b$

Trapezium area $=\frac{(2b+b)}{2}\frac{\sqrt{3}}{2}b=\frac{3\sqrt{3}}{4}b^2$

Total hexagon area $=\frac{3\sqrt{3}}{2}b^2$

So from equal volumes: $a^2 = \frac{3\sqrt{3}}{2}b^2$

Ratio: $\sqrt{\frac{3\sqrt{3}}{2}}$

Question 286: C

A cube has 6 sides so the area of 9 cm cube = 6 x 9^2

9 cm cube splits into 3 cm cubes.

Area of 3 cm cubes = 3^3 x 6 x 3^2

$\frac{6 \times 3^2 \times 3^3}{6 \times 3^2 \times 3^2} = 3$

Question 287: E

$x^2 = (4r)^2 + r^2$

$x = \sqrt{17}r$

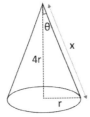

$\frac{\sqrt{17}r}{\sin 90°} = \frac{r}{\sin \theta}$

$\theta = \sin^{-1}\left(\frac{1}{\sqrt{17}}\right)$

Question 288: C

0 to 200 is 180 degrees so: $\frac{\theta}{180} = \frac{70}{200}$

$\theta = \frac{7 \times 180}{20} = 63°$

Question 289: C

Since the rhombi are similar, the ratio of angles = 1

Length scales with square root of area so length B = $\sqrt{10}$ length A

$\frac{angle\ A / angle\ B}{length\ A / length\ B} = \frac{1}{\sqrt{10}/1} = \frac{1}{\sqrt{10}}$

Question 290: E

$y = \ln(2x^2)$

$e^y = 2x^2$

$x = \sqrt{\frac{e^y}{2}}$

As the input is -x, the inverse function must be $f(x) = -\sqrt{\frac{e^y}{2}}$

Question 291: C

$log_8(x)$ and $log_{10}(x) < 0$; $x^2 < 1$; $\sin(x) \leq 1$ and $1 < e^x < 2.72$

So e^x is largest over this range

Question 292: C

$x \propto \sqrt{z}^3$

$\sqrt{2}^3 = 2\sqrt{2}$

Question 293: A

The area of the shaded part, that is the difference between the area of the larger and smaller circles, is three times the area of the smaller so: $\pi r^2 - \pi x^2 = 3\pi x^2$. From this, we can see that the area of the larger circle, radius x, must be 4x the smaller one so: $4\pi r^2 = \pi x^2$

$4r^2 = x^2$

$x = 2r$

The gap is $x - r = 2r - r = r$

Question 294: D

$x^2 + 3x - 4 \geq 0$
$(x - 1)(x + 4) \geq 0$

Hence, $x - 1 \geq 0$ or $x + 4 \geq 0$

So $x \geq 1$ or $x \geq -4$

Question 295: C

$\frac{4}{3}\pi r^3 = \pi r^2$

$\frac{4}{3}r = 1$

$r = \frac{3}{4}$

Question 296: B

When $x^2 = \frac{1}{x}$; $x = 1$

When $x > 1, x^2 > 1, \frac{1}{x} < 1$

When $x < 1, x^2 < 1, \frac{1}{x} > 1$

Range for $\frac{1}{x}$ is $x > 0$

Non-inclusive so: $0 < x < 1$

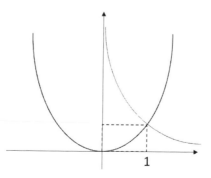

Question 297: A

Don't be afraid of how difficult this initially looks. If you follow the pattern, you get (e-e) which = 0. Anything multiplied by 0 gives zero.

Question 298: C

For two vectors to be perpendicular their scalar product must be equal to 0.

Hence, $\begin{pmatrix} -1 \\ 6 \end{pmatrix} \cdot \begin{pmatrix} 2 \\ k \end{pmatrix} = 0$

$\therefore -2 + 6k = 0$

$k = \dfrac{1}{3}$

Question 299: C

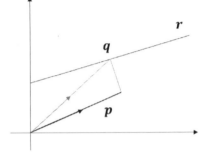

The point, q, in the plane meets the perpendicular line from the plane to the point p.

$q = -3i + j + \lambda_1(i + 2j)$

$\overrightarrow{PQ} = -3i + j + \lambda_1(i + 2j) + 4i + 5j$

$= \begin{pmatrix} -7 + \lambda_1 \\ -4 + 2\lambda_1 \end{pmatrix}$

PQ is perpendicular to the plane r therefore the dot product of $\overrightarrow{PQ}$ and a vector within the plane must be 0.

$\begin{pmatrix} -7 + \lambda_1 \\ -4 + 2\lambda_1 \end{pmatrix} \cdot \begin{pmatrix} 1 \\ 2 \end{pmatrix} = 0$

$\therefore -7 + \lambda_1 - 8 + 4 + \lambda_1 = 0$

$\lambda_1 = 3$

$\overrightarrow{PQ} = \begin{pmatrix} -4 \\ 2 \end{pmatrix}$

The perpendicular distance from the plane to point p is therefore the modulus of the vector joining the two $\overrightarrow{PQ}$:

$|\overrightarrow{PQ}| = \sqrt{(-4)^2 + 2^2} = \sqrt{20} = 2\sqrt{5}$

Question 300: E

$-1 + 3\mu = -7 \; ; \; \mu = -2$

$2 + 4\lambda + 2\mu = 2 \; \therefore \; \lambda = 1$

$3 + \lambda + \mu = k \; \therefore \; k = 2$

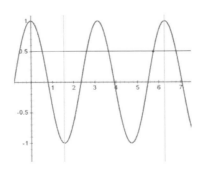

Question 301: E

$$\sin\left(\frac{\pi}{2} - 2\theta\right) = \cos(2\theta)$$

Root solution to $\cos(\theta) = 0.5$

$$\theta = \frac{\pi}{3}$$

Solution to $\cos(2\theta) = 0.5$

$$\theta = \frac{\pi}{6}$$

Largest solution within range is: $2\pi - \frac{\pi}{6} = \frac{(12-1)\pi}{6} = \frac{11\pi}{6}$

Question 302: A

$$\cos^4(x) - \sin^4(x) \equiv \{\cos^2(x) - \sin^2(x)\}\{\cos^2(x) + \sin^2(x)\}$$

From difference of two squares, then using Pythagorean identity $\cos^2(x) + \sin^2(x) = 1$

$$\cos^4(x) - \sin^4(x) \equiv \cos^2(x) - \sin^2(x)$$

But double angle formula says: $\cos(A + B) = \cos(A)\cos(B) - \sin(A)\sin(B)$

$\therefore if\ A = B, \cos(2A) = \cos(A)\cos(A) - \sin(A)\sin(A)$

$$= \cos^2(A) - \sin^2(A)$$

So, $\cos^4(x) - \sin^4(x) \equiv \cos(2x)$

Question 303: C

Factorise: $(x + 1)(x + 2)(2x - 1)(x^2 + 2) = 0$

Three real roots at $x = -1, x = -2, x = 0.5$ and two imaginary roots at 2i and -2i

Question 304: C

An arithmetic sequence has constant difference d so the sum increases by d more each time:

$$u_n = u_1 + (n - 1)d$$

$$\sum_1^n u_n = \frac{n}{2}\{2u_1 + (n - 1)d\}$$

$$\sum_1^8 u_n = \frac{8}{2}\{4 + (8 - 1)3\} = 100$$

Question 305: E

$$\binom{n}{k} 2^{n-k}(-x)^k = \binom{5}{2} 2^{5-2}(-x)^2$$

$$= 10 \times 2^3 x^2 = 80x^2$$

Question 306: A

Having already thrown a 6 is irrelevant. A fair die has equal probability $P = \frac{1}{6}$ for every throw.

For three throws: $P(6 \cap 6 \cap 6) = \left(\frac{1}{6}\right)^3 = \frac{1}{216}$

Question 307: D

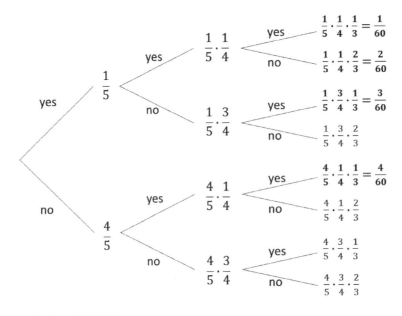

Total probability is sum of all probabilities:

$= P(Y \cap Y \cap Y) + P(Y \cap Y \cap N) + P(Y \cap N \cap Y) + P(N \cap Y \cap Y)$

$= \frac{1}{60} + \frac{2}{60} + \frac{3}{60} + \frac{4}{60} = \frac{10}{60} = \frac{1}{6}$

Question 308: C

$P[(A \cup B)'] = 1 - P[(A \cup B)]$

$= 1 - \{P(A) + P(B) - P(A \cap B)\}$

$= 1 - \frac{2+6-1}{8} = \frac{3}{8}$

Question 309: D

Using the product rule: $\frac{dy}{dx} = x \cdot 4(x+3)^3 + 1 \cdot (x+3)^4$

$= 4x(x+3)^3 + (x+3)(x+3)^3$

$= (5x+3)(x+3)^3$

Question 310: A

$$\int_1^2 \frac{2}{x^2}dx = \int_1^2 2x^{-2}\,dx =$$

$$\left[\frac{2x^{-1}}{-1}\right]_1^2 = \left[\frac{-2}{x}\right]_1^2$$

$$= \frac{-2}{2} - \frac{-2}{1} = -1$$

Question 311: D

Express $\frac{5i}{1+2i}$ in the form $a + bi$

$$\frac{5i}{1+2i} \cdot \frac{1-2i}{1-2i}$$

$$= \frac{5i+10}{1+4} - \frac{5i+10}{5}$$

$$= i + 2$$

Question 312: B

$$7\log_a(2) - 3\log_a(12) + 5\log_a(3)$$

$$7\log_a(2) = \log_a(2^7) = \log_a(128)$$

$$3\log_a(12) = \log_a(1728)$$

$$5\log_a(3) = \log_a(243)$$

This gives: $\log_a(128) - \log_a(1728) + \log_a(243)$

$$= \log_a\left(\frac{128\times243}{1728}\right) = \log_a(18)$$

Question 313: E

Functions of the form quadratic over quadratic have a horizontal asymptote.

Divide each term by the highest order in the polynomial i.e. x^2:

$$\frac{2x^2 - x + 3}{x^2 + x - 2} = \frac{2 - \frac{1}{x} + \frac{3}{x^2}}{1 + \frac{1}{x} - \frac{2}{x^2}}$$

$$\lim_{x\to\infty}\left(\frac{2 - \frac{1}{x} + \frac{3}{x^2}}{1 + \frac{1}{x} - \frac{2}{x^2}}\right) = \frac{2}{1} \quad i.e.\, y \to 2$$

So, the asymptote is $y = 2$

Question 314: A

$1 - 3e^{-x} = e^x - 3$

$4 = e^x + 3e^{-x} = \frac{(e^x)^2}{e^x} + \frac{3}{e^x} = \frac{(e^x)^2+3}{e^x}$

This is a quadratic equation in (e^x): $(e^x)^2 - 4(e^x) + 3 = 0$

$(e^x - 3)(e^x - 1) = 0$

So $e^x = 3, x = \ln(3)$ or $e^x = 1, x = 0$

Question 315: D

Rearrange into the format: $(x + a)^2 + (y + b)^2 = r^2$

$(x - 3)^2 + (y + 4)^2 - 25 = 12$

$(x - 3)^2 + (y + 4)^2 = 47$

$\therefore r = \sqrt{47}$

Question 316: C

$\sin(-x) = -\sin(x)$

$\int_0^a 2\sin(-x)\,dx = -2\int_0^a \sin(x)\,dx = -2[\cos(x)]_0^a = \cos(a) - 1$

Solve $\cos(a) - 1 = 0$ $\therefore a = 2k\pi$

Or simply the integral of any whole period of sin(x) = 0 i.e. $a = 2k\pi$

Question 317: E

$\frac{2x+3}{(x-2)(x-3)^2} = \frac{A}{(x-2)} + \frac{B}{(x-3)} + \frac{C}{(x-3)^2}$

$2x + 3 = A(x - 3)^2 + B(x - 2)(x - 3) + C(x - 2)$

When $x = 3, (x - 3) = 0$, $C = 9$

When $x = 2, (x - 2) = 0, A = 7$

$2x + 3 = 7(x - 3)^2 + B(x - 2)(x - 3) + 9(x - 2)$

For completeness: Equating coefficients of x^2 on either side: $0 = 7 + B$ which gives: $B = -7$

END OF SECTION

Final Advice

Arrive well rested, well fed and well hydrated

The ECAA is an intensive test, so make sure you're ready for it. Ensure you get a good night's sleep before the exam (there is little point cramming) and don't miss breakfast. If you're taking water into the exam then make sure you've been to the toilet before so you don't have to leave during the exam. Make sure you're well rested and fed in order to be at your best!

Move on

If you're struggling, move on. Every question has equal weighting and there is no negative marking. In the time it takes to answer on hard question, you could gain three times the marks by answering the easier ones. Be smart to score points- especially in section 1B where some questions are far easier than others.

Make Notes on your Essay

You may be asked questions on your ECAA essay at the interview. Given that there is likely to be several weeks between the test and interview, it is imperative that you make short notes on the essay title and your main arguments after the essay.

Afterword

Remember that the route to a high score is your approach and practice. Don't fall into the trap that *"you can't prepare for the ECAA"*– this could not be further from the truth. With knowledge of the test, some useful time-saving techniques and plenty of practice you can dramatically boost your score.

Work hard, never give up and do yourself justice.

Good luck!

Acknowledgements

I would like to express my sincerest thanks to the many people who helped make this book possible, especially the Oxbridge Tutors who shared their expertise in compiling the huge number of questions and answers.

Rohan

About Us

Infinity Books is the publishing division of *Infinity Education Ltd.* We currently publish over 85 titles across a range of subject areas – covering specialised admissions tests, examination techniques, personal statement guides, plus everything else you need to improve your chances of getting on to competitive courses such as medicine and law, as well as into universities such as Oxford and Cambridge.

Outside of publishing we also operate a highly successful tuition division, called UniAdmissions. This company was founded in 2013 by Dr Rohan Agarwal and Dr David Salt, both Cambridge Medical graduates with several years of tutoring experience. Since then, every year, hundreds of applicants and schools work with us on our programmes. Through the programmes we offer, we deliver expert tuition, exclusive course places, online courses, best-selling textbooks and much more.

With a team of over 1,000 Oxbridge tutors and a proven track record, UniAdmissions have quickly become the UK's number one admissions company.

Visit and engage with us at:

Website (Infinity Books): www.infinitybooks.co.uk

Website (UniAdmissions): www.uniadmissions.co.uk

Facebook: www.facebook.com/uniadmissionsuk

Twitter: @infinitybooks7

Printed in Great Britain
by Amazon

47207601R00120